P9-CMO-190

RESEARCH THAT INFORMS TEACHERS AND TEACHER EDUCATORS

by
Donald R. Cruickshank
Ohio State University

A Publication of the
PHI DELTA KAPPA
Educational Foundation
Bloomington, Indiana

Cover design by Peg Caudell

Library of Congress Catalog Card Number 90-61036
ISBN 0-87367-446-4
Copyright © 1990 by Donald R. Cruickshank

Dedication

This book is dedicated to three groups: first to its readers in the hope that they will find information herein useful in guiding professional practice; second to those persons who strive mightily to conduct research in sometimes unrewarding and hostile environments; and finally to my research colleagues, with whom I have served at the State University of New York-Brockport, University of Tennessee, and Ohio State University.

Preface

My purpose in writing this monograph is to present selected, research-based knowledge that can inform the practices of teaching and teacher preparation. To obtain the research aggregated and synthesized in this book, I read both original studies and reviews. Where a seemingly good review existed, it is summarized. Where such reviews did not exist, original studies are reported in alphabetical order by author. In some instances, the research reported did not include what one would consider to be critical information: the study's purpose, methodology (including descriptions of the sample, instruments, treatments), and even the findings. Marsh (1987) provides an enlightening discussion of the difficulty of obtaining this kind of literature and its attendant limitations.

No attempt was made to judge the quality of the research. However, since the major portion of it was published in refereed journals, it has undergone the peer review process, thus establishing some measure of credibility. The quality and generalizability of education research in general, and the research reviewed here in particular, have been thoroughly argued by others over the past several decades. Suffice it to say, almost all education research suffers some shortcomings; and seldom is much of it widely generalizable. Nevertheless, it is some of the best knowledge we have. If considered prudently, it should enlighten us in ways that can improve both teaching and teacher preparation.

By juxtaposing the models for conducting inquiry on teaching and teacher education with a synthesis of research on what we currently know, it is my hope that this book will make clear what yet we need to know and thus encourage further inquiry.

Chapter One begins with the question: Why has there been so little inquiry that informs teachers and teacher educators? One reason is that until recently no models have existed to guide such inquiry. Now, however, several models for research on teaching and teacher education do exist. They are presented here in a form that permits presentation of some of the research findings according to the categories of variables the models posit.

Chapters Two, Three, and Four summarize research that informs both teaching and teacher education with the focus on what is known about effective schools, educational practices, and teaching. This research-based knowledge is important to K-12 personnel because, within limits, it has direct application in schools. At the same time, such knowledge, within limits, has potential for teacher educators, who can use it to select preservice teachers, to design the teacher preparation curriculum, and to enhance their own instruction.

Chapter Two, "The Search for Knowledge About Effective Schools," identifies the factors that research shows contribute to school effectiveness and describes how effective school research is being done. The summaries of the most significant research allow readers to judge for themselves whether the findings are generalizable to their workplace. The chapter concludes with a discussion of some of the shortcomings of effective schools research and of how the research findings may be used by teachers and teacher educators.

Chapter Three, "The Search for Knowledge About Effective Educational Practices," presents a rationale for the importance of such investigations. It synthesizes some of the earlier research efforts to identify specific exemplary curricular and instructional practices. A major portion of the chapter is devoted to four recent reviews of research on effective K-12 educational practice. The chapter concludes with a consideration of how to use the research findings.

Chapter Four, "The Search for Knowledge About Effective Teaching," first considers the questions: What is an effective teacher? and Why is there a never-ending search for effective teachers? It then describes how inquiry on teaching has been conducted and presents some of the more significant findings. The chapter concludes with a discussion of some of the limitations of such research and how the research can be used.

Chapter Five, "The Search for Knowledge About Teacher Preparation," reviews research on teacher educaton in four categories: What we know about 1) preservice teachers, 2) curriculum and instruction, 3) members of the education professoriate, and 4) the context in which teacher preparation occurs.

Chapter Six, "Review and Recommendations," summarizes the material presented in the previous five chapters and concludes with the author's observations and recommendations for action.

Donald R. Cruickshank
Ohio State University
January 1990

References

Marsh, D. "Faculty Development for Preservice Teacher Educators: A Research Utilization Perspective." *Teaching & Teacher Education* 3, no. 4 (1987): 357-63.

Table of Contents

1 The Need for Knowledge That Informs Teachers and Teacher Educators

Many kinds of knowledge serve to inform teachers and teacher educators. Knowing about what makes a school effective is one kind. Another is knowledge of what constitutes effective educational programs and practices. A third is knowing what makes a teacher effective. These three kinds of knowledge are of direct use for K-12 practitioners. They also have value for teacher educators, since they help to define what knowlege and skills preservice and inservice teachers need to have and thus serve as a basis for developing the teacher education curriculum. A fourth kind of knowledge is about the field of teacher preparation itself. Clearly, access to these four kinds of knowledge should result in more effective K-12 teaching and improved teacher preparation programs.

Needed: Models for Guiding Inquiry in Teaching and Teacher Education

Knowledge production has not been a hallmark of the field of education. Why is this so? Perhaps it is because until recently there have been no models to guide inquiry in teaching and teacher education. Although knowledge generation in education is receiving greater attention and seems to be increasing, it has a long way to go.

If teachers and teacher educators are to have self-respect and the respect of other professionals including the general public, their preparation must be based on verified knowledge — knowledge that is held in high regard and that informs practice. Were this so, we would have no more "What do you do? I'm just a teacher" dialogues. Were this so, we would not be subjected to the kind of teacher bashing one finds in such reports as *The Miseducation of American Teachers*, *Crisis in the Classroom*, and *A Nation*

1

at Risk. Were this so, we would have no trouble deciding which books to save if the education library were on fire.

Why isn't this so? Why are the enormous enterprises of teaching (approximately two million members) and teacher education (approximately 1,200 colleges and universities preparing well over 100,000 teachers annually) not driven by an adequate body of verified knowledge? Answers can be found by looking at the history of teacher education in this country.

Historically teacher preparation was largely the responsibility of normal schools and later teachers colleges. These institutions were committed to teaching, not research. The academic faculty in these institutions were expected to teach teachers. They were not expected to engage in knowledge production, and few did so. Moreover, the professional education faculty were often doctrinaire and prone to promoting their own particular education ideology. Their classes in pedagogy amounted to little more than sharing their personal experiences along with a sprinkling of "how-to" advice. Thus for several generations preservice teachers, some of whom would themselves become teacher preparers, were not exposed to much beyond ideology and personal experience. They were taught that teaching was merely a matter of knowing your subject matter and having your heart (ideology) in the right place. The heart would guide the hand. The apprenticeship called student teaching was the culminating event in preservice teachers' preparation to see whether they could relate to children, develop a lesson plan, and manage a classroom. Said another way, there was more form than substance to the making of a teacher.

A second reason why teaching and teacher education may be less well-informed by research is the background of teacher educators. In many cases they have been successful elementary or secondary school teachers and believe they should mold future teachers in their own image. Their career goals are likely to be guided neither by theoretical interests nor by the propagation of knowledge that might inform and perhaps alter teacher preparation programs.

Once prospective teacher educators enter doctoral programs, other inhibitors are evident. Generally, they have not been exposed to research traditions as undergraduates or in their master's degree programs. Most did not have to write a master's degree thesis, so the doctoral dissertation is the first significant scholarly task they have faced. It is little wonder that they approach that task with great trepidation or that the result is often naive and held in low regard by faculty in other disciplines accustomed to seeing more sophisticated products.

To complicate matters, advisors of doctoral students in education often have done little research beyond their own dissertation and are inhibited from doing so because of heavy teaching loads and large numbers of advisees. Moreover, both doctoral students and their mentors may have no rigorous course requirements that would facilitate the conduct of inquiry. Surprisingly, there are no standards that prospective teacher educators must meet relating either to the field of teacher education or to the conduct of inquiry in the field.

Still another factor contributing to the lack of support for research that informs teaching and teacher education is the failure to reward such efforts. Although universities expect, even demand, that faculty conduct research, it frequently must be accomplished as an add-on to regular duties. Few universities, even those with research centers, give researchers reduced teaching, advising, or service responsibilities unless they can buy released time by obtaining funding outside the university. Relatedly, a research publication may be equated with simply publishing any type of article. Thus the price may be too high to engage in knowledge generation. Adding to the problem is the practice by a few select research universities of promoting their most competent and productive researchers to administrative positions.

Given the paucity of research that informs teaching and teacher preparation, it is no surprise that few outlets exist for publishing research. A researcher may have only one or two true research journals in which to place a report of a study. A rejection due to lack of journal space or even on grounds that the inquiry may have some methodological flaws can be enough to dissuade further effort.

A further limitation is the lack of funding for research on teaching and teacher education. It has been a long time since federal funding agencies have supported such inquiry in a systematic way. Unfortunately, the available funding, which is inadequate by any standard, is directed to one or two places. In the absence of research monies, schools of education cajole faculty to apply for funds available for training and dissemination activities for which, in some cases, no empirical support exists.

In addition to the above limitations and shortcomings that contribute to the relatively low status of research on teaching and teacher education, two others are noteworthy. First, there are many who believe that teaching and teacher education are just too complex phenomena to study systematically. Second, until recently there have been few models to guide research in these areas. While accepting that teaching and teacher education are complex phenomena, it does not follow, then, that researchers should not attempt to understand and explain them using a variety of models that suggest variables for study or hypotheses to test. We simply cannot accept that teaching and teacher education defy straightforward attempts to understand them.

Models with Promise to Guide Inquiry in Teaching and Teacher Education

One of the most promising developments in education is the advent of models that attempt to define the variables extant in teaching and teacher education and that suggest potential areas of inquiry that can inform teachers and teacher educators.

Dunkin and Biddle (1974) explain why creating a model to study a complex phenomenon such as teaching is important: "To set up a model for something complex is often the first step in the development of a genuine theory concerning it" (p. 31). Here a model means a preliminary representation that tries to capture the essential features of some complex phenomenon. The model attempts to account for the essential parts of a phenomenon and the relationships among the parts. Thus a model of teaching would seek to describe the major variables operating during the act of teaching, while a model of teacher education would identify the principal elements of that field and their relationships. Once a model is developed and consensus is established regarding its validity, then it can be used to guide inquiry.

Models for the study of teaching. A prototypical model of teaching was suggested by Mitzel (1960). He proposed that teaching as a phenomenon must take into account three sets of variables: teachers and pupils, their interactions, and the product of those interactions. Dunkin and Biddle (1974) expanded on Mitzel's model as shown in Figure 1.

This model, after Mitzel, presents the four major variable types: presage, context, process, and product. *Presage variables* are those that influence teachers and their teaching behavior and fall into three subtypes: formative, experiential, and properties (primarily psychological). They are the variables that a researcher can study to predict (presage) teacher behavior. The arrows on the model indicate a linear effect of the variables on each other and eventually on the teacher's classroom behavior.

Two types of *context variables* appear in the model: 1) pupil and 2) school and community. The arrows on the model indicate how pupil formative experiences influence pupil "properties" or attributes, which, in turn, influence pupil classroom behavior. The other context variable, school and community, operates in the same way, influencing the characteristics and artifacts of the classroom, which, in turn, have a bearing on teacher and pupil classroom interactions.

The *process variables* are behaviors displayed in the classroom as teachers and pupils interact. Examples of such behaviors are teacher talk and pupil response. According to the model, such interactions result in changes in pupil behavior.

Figure 1. A model for the study of classroom teaching.

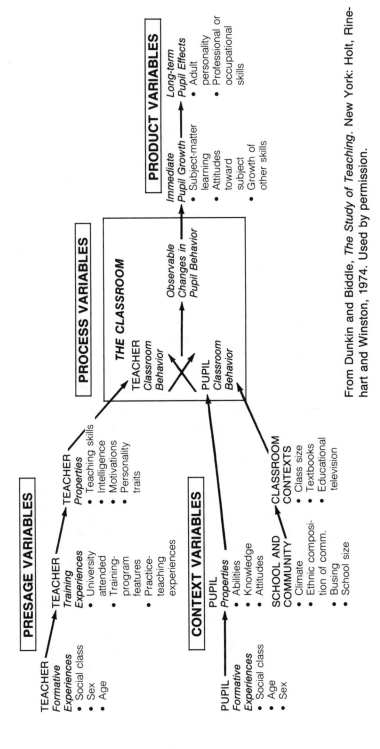

From Dunkin and Biddle, *The Study of Teaching*. New York: Holt, Rinehart and Winston, 1974. Used by permission.

5

Finally, *product variables* include the types of changes in pupil behavior that result from the process variables. These may be either immediate or long term.

The essence of this inquiry model is that three sets of input variables influence the fourth, or product variable. Further, each set of variables includes subsets, whose influence is linear and one directional. Suffice it to say, any first effort to develop an inquiry model for a phenomenon as complex as teaching is bound to be scrutinized. This has happened, and soon refinements and alternative models were proposed (Centra and Potter 1980; Doyle 1977; Erickson 1976; Fisher and Berliner 1979; Harnishfeger and Wiley 1976; McDonald and Elias 1976; Medley 1982; and Shulman 1986). Figure 2 depicts the version of a model for the study of teaching proposed by McDonald and Elias.

In this model the terms used to describe the variables have changed and new variables have been added. For example, the terms "teacher formative experiences" and "teacher training experiences" have been changed to "teacher's characteristics," "teacher's knowledge of subject," "teacher's knowledge of teaching," etc. New variables added include "organizational structure" and "principal's and teacher's perception of organization." Additionally, the model indicates (with two-way arrows) that some variables influence each other, for example, "teacher's attitudes" and "student's attitudes."

Another alternative to Mitzel and Dunkin and Biddle's process-product model is Medley's (1982) model, depicted in Figure 3 on page 8.

In his model, Medley replaces the process-product models with what he calls the "triangular design." He describes his nine-variable design thusly:

> The five cells in the top row define five types of variables, each of which has been used at one time or another as a criterion for evaluating teachers. The four cells in the second row define four additional types of variables that affect the outcomes of teaching and that are not controlled by the teacher. [Arrows indicate flow of influence.] . . . The effectiveness of a teacher [as judged by the pupil learning outcomes] depends then on at least eight other kinds of variables. . . . It is the aim of research in teacher effectiveness to clarify the contributions of all eight. . . .
>
> The general strategy for the research is to interrelate variables in adjacent cells, taking into account variables [in the lower row] that directly affect the relationship. . . .
>
> The influences of variables in any one variable [box] are assumed to exert direct influence only on variables in the cell directly connected to them by an arrow; thus pre-existing teacher characteristics and teacher training are assumed to affect teacher competence directly and to affect other variables only indirectly. (pp. 1899-1901)

6

Figure 2. A structural model of the domain of variables influencing teaching performance and children's learning.

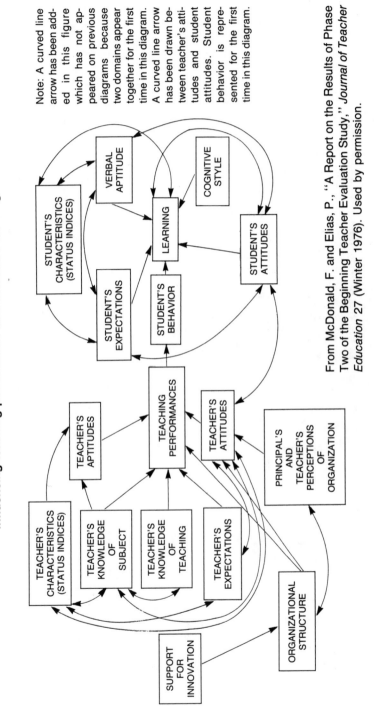

Note: A curved line arrow has been added in this figure which has not appeared on previous diagrams because two domains appear together for the first time in this diagram. A curved line arrow has been drawn between teacher's attitudes and student attitudes. Student behavior is represented for the first time in this diagram.

From McDonald, F. and Elias, P., "A Report on the Results of Phase Two of the Beginning Teacher Evaluation Study," *Journal of Teacher Education* 27 (Winter 1976). Used by permission.

Figure 3. Structure of teacher effectiveness.

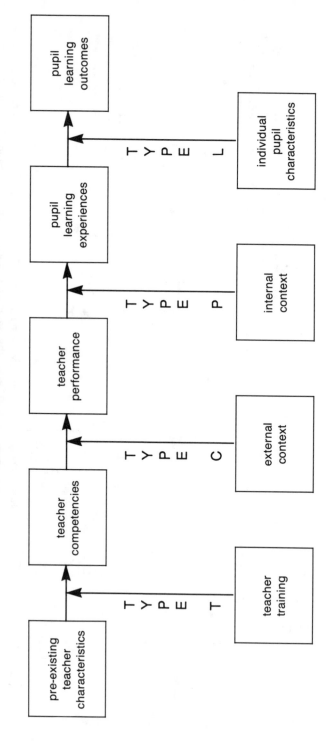

Modified from Medley, D., "Teacher Effectiveness." In *Encyclopedia of Educational Research*, edited by H. Mitzel. New York: Free Press, 1982. Used by permission.

Medley goes on to suggest four different types of research involving one of the four categories of independent variables. In Type L research, the dependent variable is any specific pupil learning outcome. The "triangular design" independent variables are the juxtaposed categories of "pupil learning experiences" and "individual pupil characteristics." In contrast to much earlier research, for Medley the unit of analysis is the pupil. The intent of Type L research is to discover what kinds of learning experiences most likely will result in the specified learning outcome with a pupil of a particular disposition.

Type P research triangulates the dependent variable, some kind of "pupil learning experiences," with the independent variables, "teacher performance" and the "internal content" (such characteristics of the teacher's class as size, average ability, ethnicity, etc.). In Type P research, the teacher is the unit of analysis, with the intent of the research being to discover which teaching strategies are most effective in providing pupils in a particular type of classroom with a specified learning experience.

Type C research triangulates the dependent measure of "teacher performance" with the independent variables "teacher competencies" and "external context" (such characteristics of the school as resources available, relationship with the community, etc.). Again, the unit of analysis is the teacher. The intent of Type C research is to discover what teacher competencies (knowledge, skills, and values) are required to implement a particular teaching strategy in a particular setting. Medley maintains that Types C, L, and P research are critical for making decisions about the objectives of teacher education and certification.

Finally, Type T research triangulates a specified "teacher competency" with "pre-existing teacher characteristics" and "teacher training." The unit of analysis here is the preservice teacher. Type T research provides insights into how to select and prepare teachers to master the competencies of effective teaching.

Each of these models (Dunkin/Biddle, McDonald/Elias, and Medley) does seem to have identified the essential elements influencing teaching and learning. They represent somewhat different perceptions of what these elements are and of their relationships; but there is enough commonality to permit researchers to isolate a goodly number of variables for study, which can lead to the improvement of teaching and the preparation of teachers.

Table 1 lists a number of the variables organized into categories, which are drawn in part from Dunkin and Biddle (Figure 1) and McDonald and Elias (Figure 2). Other variables could be added under each category.

Table 1. Variables that may infuence pupil learning and/or satisfaction.

I. Teacher Variables

A. Formative experiences
1. Social class
2. Age
3. Sex
4. Others

B. Training experiences
1. College/university attended
2. Training program emphases
3. Student teaching and other field experiences
4. Others

C. Attributes
1. Teaching aptitudes and skills
2. Intelligence
3. Motivations
4. Personality traits
5. Knowledge of subject
6. Knowledge of teaching
7. Time spent in class preparations
8. Knowledge of learners in class
9. Expectations for self and students
10. Attitudes
11. Others

II. Context Variables (conditions affecting teacher)

A. Pupil formative experiences
1. Social class
2. Age
3. Sex
4. Acceptance by others
5. Others

B. Pupil school experiences
1. Past school success
2. Number and kinds of schools attended
3. Kinds of learning experienced
   a. Discovery learning (inductive)
   b. Reception learning (deductive)
   c. Other kinds
4. Others

C. Pupil attributes
1. Abilities
2. Knowledge
3. Attitude toward school, etc.
4. Motivation
5. Awareness of and acceptance of learning objectives
6. Readiness for established curriculum
7. Perception of relevance of lessons
8. Expectations for self and others
9. Behavior
10. Cognitive style
11. Others

D. School and community contexts
1. Emotional climate
2. Ethnic composition of community
3. Busing
4. School size
5. Principal's style
6. Support for innovation
7. School organizational structure
8. Others

E. Classroom contexts
1. Class size
2. Instructional media (textbooks, television, computers)
3. Instructional time and efficient use of it.
4. Student absences and tardiness
5. Similarity of learners' abilities
6. Physical environment (temperature, lighting, noise, space, aesthetic atmosphere)
7. Others

III. Process Variables (what teachers and students do in the classroom)

A. Teacher classroom behavior/performance
1. Teacher's presentation style
   a. Clarity
   b. Variability
   c. Enthusiasm
   d. Task-oriented, businesslike behavior
   e. Opportunity to learn criterion material
   f. General indirectness, that is, use of student ideas
   g. Criticism
   h. Structuring comments

       i. Questioning techniques
       j. Level of difficulty of instruction
      k. Others
  2. Teaching strategy
    a. Didactics (direct presentational style)
    b. Heuristics (inquiry, discovery style)
    c. Philetics (personal, dealing with learners' feeling states)
  3. Using appropriate learning principles
    a. Adjusting goals for learners of different abilities
    b. Varying activities
    c. Pacing
    d. Cueing
    e. Practice
    f. Reinforcing correct responses
    g. Rewarding learners for achieving objectives
  4. Organization of content
    a. Organized logically, for example, by cognitive levels such as in Bloom's taxonomy of educational objectives
    b. Organized psychologically such as Gagne's learning hierarchy

B. Pupil learning strategies, for example, for basic learning tasks (repetition), complex tasks (copying, underlining)

C. Pupil behavior
  1. Relaxed — anxious
  2. Motivated — nonmotivated
  3. Adaptive — nonconforming
  4. Structured — unstructured
  5. On task — off task

IV. Product Variables (outcomes of teaching)

A. Immediate pupil growth
  1. Subject matter learning
  2. Attitudes toward subject matter
  3. Growth in other skills

B. Long-term pupil effects
  1. Adult personality
  2. Professional or occupational skills

With the three models of teaching presented in Figures 1, 2, and 3 and the list of promising variables in Table 1, researchers have a structure within which to to engage in several types of inquiry on teaching, namely descriptive, correlational, and experimental. To illustrate, a researcher might decide to study a teacher behavior such as "clarity." The first task would be to establish an operational definition of clarity. This could be done by asking K-12 pupils to provide anecdotal descriptions. (When this has been done, analyses of pupil descriptions of teacher clarity indicate that at the intermediate inference level they provide for pupil understanding, explain or demonstrate how to do work through the use of examples, and structure instruction and instructional content in logical ways.) Next, the researcher would spend time in the classroom to see if teacher clarity is observable using the pupil anecdotal descriptions. (In the case of clarity, it has been determined that there are 29 low-inference behaviors that identify clear teaching. Most of them have been observable, for example, "teaches step-by-step.") If it is, the researcher then would need to use some type of instrument to measure the extent to which teacher clarity is associated with pupil learning and satisfaction. (In the case of clarity, an instrument containing the clarity behaviors has been validated. Teachers' performance on the clarity instrument is compared with pupil classroom achievement. A strong, positive association has been found to exist.) Finally, if it can be shown that strong enough associations do exist, the researcher could set up an experimental study using teaching episodes in which some have clarity and some have lack of clarity. In this way it can be determined whether teacher clarity does, indeed, influence pupil outcomes. (Again with clarity, pupils intentionally would be given clear or unclear teaching, and the effects of that teaching on their achievement would be measured.)

Models for the study of teacher education. As with models for the study of teaching, there are models evolving for the study of teacher education. Cruickshank (1984) offers one model shown in Figure 4 on page 14. It uses six variables: 1) teacher educators, 2) preservice teacher education students, 3) contexts where teacher preparation takes place, 4) content of the teacher preparation curriculum, 5) instruction in the teacher preparation program, and 6) student outcomes. Each of the first five variables influence to some degree the sixth, the outcome or response variable.

In the model, teacher educators (1) include all those involved in preservice teacher preparation including education professors, academic professors, and cooperating teachers in K-12 schools. Teacher education students (2) are those involved in the preservice program. These two groups interact in the contexts (3) of teacher preparation, which include the college/university campus, K-12 schools, and community agencies if used. These interactions revolve around the preservice teacher education curriculum (4) including professional studies, on-campus and off-campus clini-

Figure 4. A model showing relationships among the primary variables extant in the field of teacher education.

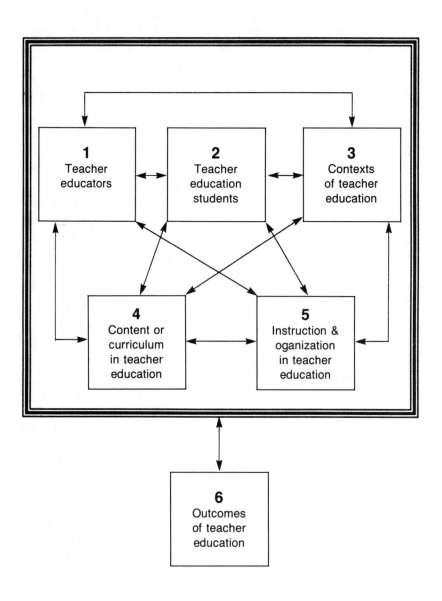

From Cruickshank, D., "Toward a Model to Guide Inquiry in Preservice Teacher Education." *Journal of Teacher Education* (1984). Used by permission.

cal and laboratory experiences, and general education. The interactions related to instruction in teacher education (5) revolve around the nature of the instructional experiences; that is, whether they are real, vicarious, or abstract (Cruickshank 1985). The outcome variable (6) sought is the preparation of able teachers who can foster pupil learning and satisfaction, however defined.

The two-way arrows indicate the reciprocal nature of the interactions. For example, it is assumed that teacher educators influence preservice teacher education students and they, in turn, influence teacher educators.

Table 2 offers a further breakdown of the five principal explanatory variables posited to exist in the field of teacher education. This list is not inclusive; other variable categories could be added.

Table 2. Explanatory variables within the field of teacher education and suggested subcategories.

I. **Teacher Educators**

   A. Formative influence
      1. Family background
      2. Socioeconomic background
      3. Education background
      4. Others

   B. Personal characteristics and abilities
      1. Activity/energy level
      2. Physical/mental status
      3. Expectations of self, program, teaching
      4. Self-confidence
      5. Academic success
      6. Social success
      7. Values/attitudes
      8. Others

   C. Professional characteristics and abilities
      1. Ability to bring about achievement and satisfaction in preservice students
      2. Ability to teach preservice students the behaviors requisite for bringing about pupil achievement and satisfaction in K-12 classrooms
      3. Ability to establish mutually satisfactory relationships with professional colleagues
      4. Level of interest in teaching teachers
      5. Knowledge of subject
      6. Others

   D. Teaching styles, behaviors

II. Preservice students

A. Formative influences
   1. Family background
   2. Sex
   3. Socioeconomic background
   4. Life experiences, work, hobbies
   5. Education background (schools attended, programs taken, academic achievement)
   6. Mental abilities
   7. Others

B. Personal characteristics and abilities
   1. Age
   2. Sex
   3. Socioeconomic status
   4. Activity/energy level
   5. Physical/mental status
   6. Self-confidence
   7. Academic success to date
   8. Success in peer relationships
   9. Values and attitudes toward schooling and learning
   10. Learning styles
   11. Others

II. Context of teacher education on campus and in the field

A. Institutional characteristics
   1. Size
   2. Composition
   3. Organization including administration-to-faculty ratio
   4. Leadership style
   5. Fiscal support and services provided
   6. Rewards provided
   7. Emotional climate

B. Classroom characteristics
   1. Physical condition (size, temperature, lighting, aesthetic atmosphere)
   2. Equipment
   3. Others

IV. Content of teacher education curriculum

A. Sources
   1. State government
   2. Federal government
   3. School districts and teachers in those districts

16

4. Schools or departments of education in college/universities
5. Teacher unions (NEA, AFT)
6. Teacher education professional associations (ATE, AACTE)
7. Accrediting agencies (NCATE) and learned societies (NCTE, NCSS, NCTM, etc.)
8. Naturalistic events (social change, etc.)
9. Individual teacher educators
10. Philanthropic foundations

B. Nature of content
1. General education
2. Professional education
   a. Content for teaching specialty
   b. Education in the undergirding disciplines of education (psychology, sociology)
   c. Teaching and learning theory
   d. Humanistic and behavioral studies (foundations area)
   e. Practicums of various sorts

C. Amount of content

D. Order or sequence of content

V. Instruction and instructional organization in teacher education

A. Instructional alternatives
1. Direct experience teaching in natural classrooms
2. Direct experience teaching in on-campus settings such as microteaching, simulations, and reflective teaching
3. Vicarious experience using protocol materials
4. Vicarious experience using films and novels about teaching
5. Abstract experiences using reading and discussion about teaching

B. Organization for instruction
1. Independent learning such as programmed instruction, computer-assisted instruction, tutoring
2. Interactive group experiences such as team learning
3. Whole-class activity

C. Student-teacher ratio

Other models that illuminate and promote inquiry in the field of teacher education are those of Zimpher and Ashburn (1985) and Katz and Rath (1985). Zimpher and Ashburn suggest the variables of teacher education students, teacher preparation units, teacher preparation programs (including faculty, curriculum, instruction), program outcomes, teaching, and pupils. A limitation of their model is that because it lacks narrative description, some variables are unclear; and no attention is given to the interrelationships among the variables. Katz and Rath offer what they call the "parameters of teacher education programs." The parameters include goals, candidates, staff, content, methods, time, ethos, regulations, resources, evaluation, and impact. This model does offer a narrative description and thus comparisons can be made with the Cruickshank model. Such comparison suggests the possible addition of goals, regulations, and evaluation to the Cruickshank model.

In the Katz/Rath model, goals are described as to their nature, explicitness, and acceptance. Regulations are described as the requirements that students must meet to graduate and to be certified, or that an institution's programs must meet to be approved by state agencies or accredited by the National Council for Accreditation of Teacher Education. Evaluation refers to the efforts to assess the extent to which the program is achieving its goals and whether the goals are valid. For example, are graduates competent when they go out into the field? The other Katz/Rath parameters are identical to Cruickshank's six variables or subsumed within one of them.

As with research on teaching, inquiry in teacher preparation can be descriptive, correlational, and experimental. To illustrate, by taking the variable "teacher educator" and a characteristic thereof, such as the ability to engender reflection in preservice teachers, first we would need to describe precisely what teacher educators do when they encourage preservice teachers to be reflective. Preservice teachers would serve as informants to obtain this descriptive data. Next, we would see whether that teacher educator behavior is correlated strongly with preservice teacher learning and satisfaction. If so, then a controlled, experimental study can be done to determine whether preservice teachers working with teacher educators who engender reflection learn more and are more satisfied than are preservice teachers who do not.

Summing Up

Inquiry on effective schooling, educational practices, teaching, and teacher education is essential to improving the practice of two million K-12 teachers and to the preparation of more than 100,000 persons graduating from preservice programs each year. Unfortunately, such inquiry is seriously lacking due to a number of conditions that are difficult to overcome. However, through the use of one of more of the models described in this chapter, it is now possible to conduct inquiry into these complex phenomena.

References

Centra, J., and Potter, D. "School and Teacher Effects." *Review of Educational Research* 50, no. 2 (1980): 272-91.

Cruickshank, D. *Models for the Preparation of America's Teachers*. Bloomington, Ind.: Phi Delta Kappa Educational Foundation, 1985.

Cruickshank, D. "Toward a Model to Guide Inquiry in Preservice Teacher Education." *Journal of Teacher Education* 35, no. 6 (1984): 43-48.

Doyle, W. "Paradigms for Research on Teacher Effectiveness." In *Review of Research in Education*, Vol. 5, edited by L.S. Shulman. Itaska, Ill.: F.E. Peacock, 1977.

Dunkin, M.J., and Biddle, B.J. *The Study of Teaching*. New York: Holt, Rinehart and Winston, 1974. (Reprinted in 1982 by the University Press of America, Washington, D.C.)

Erickson, D.A. "Implications for Organizational Research of the Harnishfeger-Wiley Model." Paper presented at the annual meeting of the American Educational Research Association in San Francisco, April 1976.

Fisher, C., and Berliner, D. "Clinical Inquiry in Research on Classroom Teaching and Learning." *Journal of Teacher Education* 30, no. 6 (1979): 43-48.

Harnishfeger, A., and Wiley, D. "The Teaching-Learning Process in Elementary Schools: A Synoptic View." *Curriculum Inquiry* 6, no.1 (1976): 5-43.

Katz, L., and Rath, J. "A Framework for Research on Teacher Education Programs." *Journal of Teacher Education* 36, no. 6 (1985): 9-15.

McDonald, F., and Elias, P. "A Report on the Results of Phase II of the Beginning Teacher Evaluation Study." *Journal of Teacher Education* 27, no. 4 (1976): 316-20.

Medley, D. "Teacher Effectiveness." In *Encyclopedia of Educational Research*, 5th Ed., edited by H. Mitzel. New York: Free Press, 1982.

Mitzel, H.E. "Teacher Effectiveness." In *Encyclopedia of Educational Research*, 3rd Ed., edited by C.W. Harris. New York: Macmillan, 1960.

Shulman, L.S. "Paradigms and Research Programs in the Study of Teaching." In *Handbook of Research on Teaching*, 3rd Ed., edited by M.C. Wittrock. New York: Macmillan, 1986.

Zimpher, N., and Ashburn, E. "Studying the Professional Development of Teachers." *Journal of Teacher Education* 36, no. 6 (1985): 16-26.

2 The Search for Knowledge About Effective Schools

Perhaps the single event precipitating a flurry of research related to teaching and schooling was the publication in 1966 of *Equality of Educational Opportunity* (U.S. Department of Health, Education and Welfare), commonly referred to as *The Coleman Report* after its chief investigator, James Coleman. This research was undertaken at the behest of Congress in response to Section 402 of the Civil Rights Act of 1964, which required that a survey of elementary and secondary schools be undertaken "concerning the lack of availability of equal educational opportunity by reason of race, color or religion." Four questions determined the type of data collected for this study: 1) To what extent are racial and ethnic groups segregated? 2) Do schools offer equal educational opportunity? 3) How much are pupils learning as measured by performance on achievement tests? 4) What relationships exist between pupil achievement and the kinds of schools they attend? In the context of this chapter, the last question is the most important one to pursue.

Most everyone agrees that schools and teachers *do* make a difference in the lives of children. Generally, children who attend school regularly and longer achieve more in school and in life. But for the researcher, the critical question is, "Does going to a particular school or having a particular teacher make a difference?" Conventional wisdom says that it does, and Coleman found that this seemed to be true. However, when he investigated why this was true, he found, not surprisingly, that what accounted for most of the differences in pupil achievement among schools was attributable to one factor, the socioeconomic status (SES) of the pupils and the community. In other words, pupil achievement is closely tied to SES.

What was surprising and disconcerting to many educators was Coleman's finding that standard measures of school quality (class size, quality of textbooks, physical plant, teachers' experience, library size, etc.) affected pupil achievement very little. Thus according to the report, schools bring little influence to bear on a child's achievement that is independent of (not related to) that child's socioeconomic background. Said another way, pupils in high SES communities consistently out-perform their counterparts in low SES communities, even when special efforts are made to improve conditions in the latter.

Reanalysis of the Coleman data by Jencks et al. (1972) and a more recent study by Walberg and Fowler (1987) similarly found that SES "overwhelms all other variables in its power to predict student achievement" (Bracey 1988, p. 376). Thus pupil achievement mostly seems to be determined by chance (where and to whom a child is born). This factor looms monumentally and seems inherently unfair.

Coleman also reported that schools with pupils of similar SES composition achieve similarly. That is, within similar SES schools he found little difference among pupils' achievement scores on tests of verbal fluency, reading comprehension, and math skills. In other words, one high, medium, or low SES school seems to be about as good as another in terms of influencing pupil achievement. Coleman makes the point clearly:

> The first finding is that the schools are remarkably similar in the effect they have on the achievement of their pupils when the socioeconomic background of the pupils is taken into account. It is known that socioeconomic factors bear a strong relationship to academic achievement. When these factors are statistically controlled, however, it appears that differences between schools account for only a small fraction of differences in pupil achievement. (p. 30)

However, Coleman goes on to say:

> Improving the school of a minority pupil will increase his achievement more than will improving the school of a white child improve his. In short, whites and to a lesser extent Oriental Americans are less affected one way or the other by the quality of their schools than are minority pupils. (p. 30)

According to Coleman, when SES is controlled the other dissimilarities among schools account for only a small amount of the differences in pupil academic achievement. But not to be overlooked are the characteristics that accounted for the small difference. What are they? Coleman points to several: the quality of teachers (their verbal skills, level of education, and level of education of their parents), the educational aspirations of pupils, the pupils' sense of efficacy (having some control over their destiny), and, to a lesser

21

extent, the existence of science laboratories in the school. With regard to the differences, Coleman noted that minority pupils, with the exception of Asian Americans, are further disadvantaged by having teachers of less "quality" and by having lower educational aspirations and a lower sense of efficacy.

Responses to the Coleman Report

From the accounts of the Coleman study reported in newspapers and journals, the general public might well have concluded that schools and teachers did not make much of a difference in the achievement of students. Consequently, educators and researchers were quick to launch a rebuttal to Coleman's findings. Such rebuttal was presented, among other places, in *Do Teachers Make a Difference?* (Bureau of Educational Personnel Development 1970). This report called for improved, more accurate models and equations of school effectiveness variables and for direct observation of teacher and pupil classroom behavior to determine precisely what it is that teachers do that relates to pupil achievement and satisfaction. Specifically, the chapter by James Guthrie reports results of 19 studies done prior to 1970 wherein investigators tried to "prohibit student socioeconomic (SES) related factors from contaminating the analysis of school service effects" or to partial out the "variance accounted for by the SES of parents" (p. 32). Guthrie concludes that there is a substantial degree of consistency in the findings from the 19 studies:

> The strongest findings by far are those which relate to the number and quality of the professional staff, particularly teachers. Fifteen of the [22] studies we review find teacher characteristics, such as verbal ability, amount of experience, salary level, amount and type of academic preparation, degree level, job satisfaction, and employment status (tenured or untenured), to be significantly associated with one or more measures of pupil performance. (p. 45)

Guthrie's summary of research represented a more optimistic report. It bolstered the view of educators that schools and teachers can and do make a difference, and it spurred researchers skeptical of Coleman's findings to initiate further inquiry. The thrust of this research was to identify mostly low SES urban schools that seemed to be succeeding and to study the characteristics of these schools that seemed to be associated with their success. If schools having these characteristics were successful in overcoming the effects of poverty on their pupil populations, then they could be considered exemplary; and perhaps other schools could be helped to become more like them.

Conducting Effective Schools Research

Researchers have used different criteria when judging whether a school is effective. One group of researchers that includes Klitgaard and Hall (1974), New York State (1974), Madden et al. (1976), Austin (1978), Edmonds and Frederickson (1978), Wellisch et al. (1978), Rutter et al. (1979), California Assembly Office of Research (1984), Hallinger and Murphy (1985), and Stedman (1987) defined effective schools as those in which pupils achieved significantly above average on tests of basic skills compared to similar schools or to schools that had scored near or even above national norms for several years. These effective schools were termed "overachievers" or "outliers" in that they produced more pupil learning than normal for similar schools and, in some cases, even more than for higher SES schools.

Like Coleman, another group of researchers analyzed randomly selected schools across all SES populations looking for relationships between input factors and output factors. For example, Brookover et al (1979) studied relationships between school personnel, school social structure, and climate on pupil achievement, self-concept, and self-reliance. These relationships were studied in 91 schools with data aggregated across all schools, in majority black schools, and in majority white schools. Biniaminov and Glasman (1983), Harnisch (1985), Saka (1989), and Yelton, Miller, and Ruscoe (1989) used similar research strategies.

A third group of researchers exemplified by Weber (1971) asked for nominations of schools judged effective by others and studied them. Finally Edmonds (1979) and Brookover and Lezotte (1979) identified and examined schools that improved over time and compared them with schools that did not.

What Have We Learned from Effective Schools Research?

Following are summaries of 22 effective school studies presented in chronological order. It is important to note that these studies examine many different variables in different contexts. For example, Weber was interested in effectiveness of teaching reading in elementary inner-city schools, while Harnisch sought to determine general factors related to effective high schools. Taken as a whole, these studies can enlighten both inservice and preservice teachers as to what makes schools effective. However, readers are cautioned to be mindful of the correspondence between the samples studied and their workplace before drawing any implications for their own school or teaching practices.

Study 1. Weber (1971)

Purpose: To determine characteristics of inner-city elementary schools successful in teaching beginning reading.

Sample: Third grades with very poor children in four inner-city schools: two in New York City, one in Kansas City, and one in Los Angeles. These were selected from 95 nominated nationally as being truly "inner city" and successful in teaching beginning reading according to an independent test Weber administered. The third-grade median reading achievement scores in each of the four schools was equal to or exceeded the national average, and the percentage of nonreaders in them was unusually low.

Method: Observational information obtained during two, three-day visits to each of these schools.

Findings: Eight school and program characteristics were noted across the four schools:

1. strong leadership,
2. high expectations,
3. good atmosphere (orderly climate, sense of purpose, relatively quiet, pleasure in learning),
4. emphasis on reading,
5. extra reading personnel,
6. use of phonics,
7. individualization (modification of assignments), and
8. careful and frequent evaluation of pupil progress.

Conclusion: Within limits, the attributes of effective schools can be generalized.

Study 2. Klitgaard and Hall (1974)

Purpose: To identify schools most successful in teaching math and beginning reading across grade levels.

Sample: Fourth- and seventh-grade pupils in Michigan, second- through sixth-grade pupils in New York City, Project Talent high school pupils.

Method: Reading and math achievement scores on standardized tests were examined to see if, over the years, certain schools (controlled for SES) produced more achievement than chance would predict.

Findings: Eight of 161 Michigan schools were considered outstanding, that is, overachieving. Most were rural. Thirty of 627 schools in New York City were outstanding. However, the attributes of these schools were not reported.

Conclusion: Outstanding schools can be identified according to criteria employed. They will be few in number.

Study 3. New York Office of Education Performance Review (1974)

Purpose: To identify factors that may influence reading success in urban elementary schools.

Sample: Two New York City elementary schools in Manhattan, one relatively high achieving, one low achieving in reading. Schools were matched for median family income, percentage of families on welfare, pupil ethnicity, percentage of pupils eligible for free lunch, and pupil mobility.

Method: Case study.

Findings: Factors associated with the high achieving school were:

1. positive principal-teacher interaction,
2. frequent informal classroom observation by principal,
3. set of guidelines for schoolwide practices in reading instruction,
4. attention given to atmosphere conducive to learning, and
5. open communication with parents and community.

Study 4. Madden et al. (1976)

Purpose: To identify attributes that differentiate more effective elementary schools from less effective ones in California.

Sample: 21 pairs of elementary schools matched on the basis of pupil characteristics but differing on standardized achievement measures.

Method: (indeterminable from my source)

Findings: In the more effective schools:

1. teachers reported receiving more support,
2. there was an atmosphere conducive to learning,
3. principal had more influence on educational decision making,
4. there was more monitoring of pupil progress, and
5. there was more emphasis on achievement.

Study 5. Coulson (1977)

Purpose: To study the impact of Emergency School Aid Act (ESAA) programs designed to overcome the isolation of minority pupils during desegregation.

Sample: Schools across U.S. involved in racial desegregation.

Method: (indeterminable from my source)

Findings: Improved achievement in desegregated schools was more likely to be found where principals:

1. felt strongly about instruction;
2. communicated their instructional viewpoints to teachers in discussions and conferences after classroom observation;

3. took a dominant role in program planning, evaluation, and selecting instructional materials; and
4. emphasized and maintained academic standards.

Study 6. Austin (1978)

Purpose: To determine distinguishing characteristics of higher and lower achieving schools.

Sample: 30 "outlier" schools (18 high achieving, 12 low achieving) selected using statewide accountability data.

Method: (indeterminable from my source)

Findings: In higher achieving schools, principals:

1. were stronger leaders, participating more fully in instruction;
2. had higher expectations for themselves, teachers, and pupils; and
3. were oriented toward cognitive rather than affective goals.

Study 7. Edmonds and Frederickson (1978)

Purpose: To determine attributes of effective schools serving poor children.

Sample: The main sample was 20 elementary schools in Detroit's Model Cities Neighborhood.

Method: Analysis of data from the 20 Detroit schools, reanalysis of 1966 Equal Educational Opportunity Survey, analysis of differences between seven effective and six less effective elementary schools in Lansing, Michigan. Data from the Detroit schools was juxtaposed with other data to generate the findings.

Findings: Effective schools are characterized by leaders who:

1. promote an atmosphere that is orderly without rigidity, quiet without repression, conducive to the business at hand;
2. frequently monitor pupil progress;
3. require staff to take responsibility for instructional effectiveness;
4. set clear goals and learning objectives;
5. have a plan for resolving achievement problems in reading and math: and
6. demonstrate strong leadership, management, and instructional skills.

Study 8. Wellisch et al. (1978)

Purpose: To evaluate the impact of the Emergency School Aid Act (ESAA).

Sample: (indeterminable from my source)

Method: Leader behavior in nine elementary schools that made significant gains in reading and mathematics achievement was compared to leader behavior in 13 less effective schools.

Findings: In successful schools, teachers reported that their principals:

1. felt strongly about instruction, had definite views, and promoted those
   views;
2. regularly reviewed and discussed teacher performance;
3. felt responsible for decisions regarding instruction, selecting instructional materials, and planning programs for the entire school; and
4. provided extensive coordination of instructional programs or delegated
   others to do so.

Study 9. Brookover et al. (1979)

Purpose: To determine the importance of certain inputs on school
outcomes.

Sample: Primarily fourth- and fifth-grade pupils in 68 randomly selected
schools in Michigan.

Method: Looked for relationships between and among school input variables (personnel, school social structure characteristics, and school climate
characteristics) on school outcome variables (achievement in math/reading
at fourth grade, self-concept, academic ability, and self-reliance). The measure of achievement was performance on the Michigan School Assessment
Test (mostly reading and math).

Findings: They are numerous and include:

1. Most of the differences among schools in terms of achievement in
   math and reading and pupil self-concept, perception of academic ability, and self-reliance are explained by the following factors:
   a. personnel inputs (pupil SES, racial composition of the school,
      teacher salaries, teacher experience and advanced education,
      teacher tenure in the present school, school size, average daily
      attendance, and pupil-professional staff ratio);
   b. school social structure characteristics (teacher satisfaction, par-
      ent involvement, principal involvement in instruction, openness
      of the school's organization, personalization and individualiza-
      tion of instruction); and
   c. school climate characteristics (pupil efficacy, pupil perception
      of others' expectations and evaluations of them, principals' per-
      ception of their own and others' perception of behavior).
2. The above is even more true in majority black schools.

3. The most powerful indicators are SES; racial composition; and pupil, teacher, and principal perceptions of expectations.
4. In black schools only, teacher salary, experience and degrees, class size, and parent involvement contribute positively to achievement.

Conclusions: The expectations of teachers and principals affect pupil achievement positively. Certain low SES schools do well when the school climate is favorable; that is, when schools assume all pupils can learn, they expect all pupils to learn. They reinforce learning and they re-teach when necessary.

Study 10. Brookover and Lezotte (1979)

Purpose: To determine relationships among school social structure, school climate, and programmatic or personnel changes and their effect on consistent patterns of improvement or decline in reading achievement.
Sample: Eight elementary schools, of which six were "improving" and two were "declining."
Method: Case study.
Findings: In improving schools, principals were more likely:

1. to be instructional leaders,
2. to be assertive in that role,
3. to be disciplinarians, and
4. to assume responsibility for evaluating achievement of basic instructional objectives.

In declining schools, principals:

1. were more permissive,
2. emphasized informal relationships with teachers,
3. put more emphasis on public relations and less on evaluating instruction in basic skills.

Study 11. Edmonds (1979)

Purpose: To determine differences in leadership between "improving" and "maintaining/declining" schools.
Sample: Nine elementary schools in New York City that demonstrated substantial improvement in reading achievement over a four-year period were matched with "maintaining/declining" schools.
Method: (not identifiable from my source).
Findings: Teachers in improving schools reported:

1. effective instructional coordination within grade and schoolwide,
2. regular administrative response to teacher problems,
3. useful faculty meetings,
4. staff interaction on curriculum,
5. adequate inservice training,
6. effective communication with principals, and
7. orderly school atmosphere.

Study 12. Rutter et al. (1979)

Purpose: To determine similarities and differences among secondary schools serving like urban populations and to determine which school characteristics were associated with academic and social success.

Sample: 20 inner-city secondary schools in London, England.

Method: Prior to entering secondary school, 10-year-olds were assessed for their intellectual level, reading attainment, school behavior, and family background. Four years later the same pupils were assessed in terms of their achievement and delinquency rates.

Findings:

1. The 20 schools differed significantly in input. For example, some schools admitted many more boys with reading and behavior problems.
2. There also were differences in output. For example, schools with the most advantaged pupils were not necessarily those with the best outcomes.
3. Even among schools with similar inputs, there were significant differences in outcomes.

Conclusion: School factors affect pupil behavior and achievement.

Study 13. Rutter et al. (1979)

Purpose: To study 12 of the inner-city schools from the sample above in greater depth.

Sample: 12 of the 20 London secondary schools from Study 12.

Method: One-week observations in each school in average-ability, third-year classes. Lessons were tape-recorded and pupils responded to questionnaires. The classroom observations and tape-recorded lessons were analyzed with attention to: whether the focus was on subject matter, pupil behavior, or some other activity; whether the teacher interacted with the class and, if so, with the whole class or with individuals; use of praise or punishment; expression by teacher of positive or negative feelings toward pupils; task engagement by pupils; frequency of off-task pupil behaviors; and playground behavior. These data were compared to five outcome measures: attendance, pupil behavior, achievement, employment, and delinquency.

Findings:

1. Schools that had received the most disruptive pupils from primary schools did not necessarily have the worst classroom behavior.
2. Schools that had frequent homework assignments tended to have higher achievement, although the overall amount of homework assigned was not great.
3. Higher teacher expectations correlated positively with better attendance and higher achievement.
4. The proportion of the week devoted to teaching was associated with higher pupil achievement.
5. Teachers in more successful schools spent a higher proportion of time with the whole class.
6. Schools where lessons started promptly had better outcomes and better pupil behavior.
7. Reward, including praise, tended to be more associated with positive pupil outcomes than did punishment.
8. In schools with better attendance and academic achievement, pupils reported they could talk to staff about personal matters.
9. Schools in which a higher proportion of pupils had school responsibilities had better classroom behavior and academic success.
10. In general, individual schools performed about the same on all outcome measures. For example, schools in which pupils had above average attendance also had above average achievement and behavior.

Conclusion: Secondary schools with selected characteristics do influence pupil behavior, achievement, and attendance.

Study 14. Venesky and Winfield (1979)

Purpose: To determine the factors contributing to academic achievement in schools serving low SES pupils.

Sample: Two elementary schools in an industrial city in the Atlantic coastal area serving primarily low SES pupils that were determined to be successful at teaching reading.

Method: Data were gathered through extensive interviews, classroom observations, and analyses of school records, principals' memos, and reading specialists' logs. These data were integrated with data from similar studies of low SES, high achieving schools.

Findings: Three primary factors related to success in teaching reading were:

1. an achievement orientation by the principal or another influential person in the school district,
2. consistency of instruction across grade levels, and
3. buildingwide focus on adapting instruction to student needs.

Study 15. Biniaminov and Glasman (1983)

Purpose: To determine the influence of a few school variables on pupil achievement in secondary schools in Israel.

Sample: Stratified random sampling of 32 of 572 secondary schools in Israel. Stratification was based on public-private ownership, type of school (academic or vocational), and size/location of the town.

Method: Correlations were made to investigate the relationship between a small set of school organizational factors and pupil achievement. The factors included: the level of disadvantaged pupils in a school, the proportion of school monies provided and actually spent directly on the disadvantaged, and teachers' length of experience in the same school. The measure of pupil achievement was the proportion of 12th-graders successful in attaining a government certificate (diploma).

Findings: Teachers' length of experience in the same school seems to be the only input variable positively and directly associated with the outcome variable, attaining a government certificate. School officials tend to spend money on facilities, equipment, small class size, and extracurricular activities. Schools receiving more money because they have more disadvantaged pupils spend proportionally less of it directly on those pupils. Other relationships are weak.

Study 16. California Assembly Office of Research (1984)

Purpose: To determine the attributes of effective high schools enrolling low-ability pupils.

Sample: 79 California high schools enrolling low-ability students.

Method: A comparison was made of two subsets of 79 high schools enrolling low-ability pupils. The first subset of 58 schools enrolled a high proportion of pupils with very limited reading ability and chronic truancy. The second subset of 21 schools also enrolled low-ability pupils — although a smaller proportion — but was significantly more successful in graduating pupils able to enter the workforce or college.

Findings:

1. Low achieving schools tended to have more than 1,500 students and be located in inner cities with large Hispanic and black populations. Students' families were low SES, with 36% on welfare. About 80% to 90% of pupils were reading at 4th- to 5th-grade levels.
2. The faculty at higher achieving schools "shared a common sense of purpose," which guided curriculum development and influenced classroom and administrative procedures.
3. Teachers at higher achieving schools diagnosed pupil strengths/weaknesses at entry and used the diagnoses for assigning pupils to programs that targeted needed skills.
4. At higher achieving schools faculty reviewed the curriculum regularly and tried to expand it to include vocational training, art, drama, music, and foreign language.

Study 17. Hallinger and Murphy (1985)

Purpose: To identify factors that are associated with successful reading programs in two overachieving elementary schools.

Sample: Two elementary schools in California (one middle class, one upper-middle class) that were considered instructionally effective based on pupil performance on an annual statewide test during the California Assessment Program. For three consecutive years reading achievement in these schools exceeded expectations based on the socioeconomic background of students.

Method: Two days were spent collecting data at each school. Teachers and principals were interviewed. Classroom observations focused on specific classroom practices: direct instruction, type of behavior management, reward system, student involvement, curriculum, frequency and extent of teacher monitoring, and provision of feedback on student progress and homework. School documents such as school handbooks were inspected. Teachers, students, parents, and principals were surveyed to elicit their perceptions of the educational program.

Findings:

1. School policies and practices supported reading instruction.
2. One-and-a-half hours per day were given to reading and language arts activities.
3. All students received 50 minutes of teacher-directed reading instruction.
4. Teachers described numerous efforts to integrate reading instruction with content studies.
5. Each school used a single (although different) basal reading series.

6. Teachers used additional reading materials such as skill building materials and literature books.
7. Several teachers developed remedial programs to supplement or replace the basal series.
8. Students frequently read during free time. When assignments were completed, students could go to the library to sign out a book. Also, classrooms had a supply of books at various levels of difficulty.
9. Schools had full-time librarians who supported classroom instruction.
10. All classes went to the library weekly.
11. Students kept logs of books they read and were recognized for reaching milestones.
12. Both oral and written book reports were used.
13. Homework focused on reading and was assigned every weeknight.
14. Reading classes were not interrupted.
15. Parents were expected to attend conferences twice a year.
16. Teachers reported the reading program was coherent and coordinated.
17. Someone in each school, the principal or "faculty leaders," provided leadership to the reading program.

Study 18. Harnisch (1985)

Purpose: To determine factors associated with effective high schools.

Sample: 18,000 public high school pupils who completed a battery of academic skill tests in 1980 as sophomores and then took the same battery in 1982 as seniors.

Method: A number of instruments were used to collect data from school administrators regarding school characteristics and instructional practices. Also, instruments were used to collect information from students. All data were subjected to statistical correlations.

Findings:

1. Schools with more high SES pupils tend to obtain higher test scores.
2. Schools with greater academic emphasis tend to have higher achievement scores.
3. Schools reporting fewer discipline problems show greater achievement gains.
4. Number of courses pupils take (beyond remedial courses) is positively associated with higher test scores in the senior year.
5. Pupils with a high sense of efficacy (feel responsible for personal success or failure) have higher verbal, science, and composite test scores.

Study 19. Stedman (1987)

Purpose: To identify low inference descriptions of school practices associated with "remarkable schools."

Sample: Public schools located mostly in impoverished communities that had "turned in remarkable performances" and that had for several years scored near or above national norms.

Method: Analysis of case studies appearing in the effective schools literature that, for the most part, provided detailed descriptions of school organization and practices.

Findings:

1. Schools acknowledged and fostered the ethnic and racial identity of pupils.
2. Schools communicated with and involved parents.
3. Teams of teachers and parents shared in school governance.
4. Programs were academically rich, varied, and demanding.
5. Teachers were strategically assigned with the best teachers targeted for lower grades or involved in remedial work. On-the-job inservice training was utilized extensively.
6. Pupils were provided close, personal attention by using volunteers (thus lowering pupil-teacher ratios), ability grouping, before- and after-school tutoring, and by increasing time devoted to certain subjects.
7. Pupils were given responsibility for day-to-day school activities including cafeteria supervision, school ground cleanup, safety, etc.
8. Good behavior resulted from effective school organization and positive learning environments rather than from the imposition of rules and rigid discipline.
9. Schools tried to head off academic problems by providing special instruction promptly and by alerting parents early if learning problems arose.

Study 20. Miller et al. (1988)

Purpose: Part of a larger effort to determine what factors might be associated with school retention and dropout of at-risk pupils.

Sample: Six male students — three learning disabled (LD) and three non-learning disabled randomly selected from 10th- and 11th-grade pupils in regular and vocational education tracks in an unidentified junior-senior high school located in a blue-collar community of 24,000. The community is 63% white and has an average family income of $17,000.

Method: Target pupils, their teachers, and classes were observed in English, math, and social studies for three consecutive days each month between November 1986 and May 1987. Data were collected for a total of 59 observations in special education classrooms and 152 regular classrooms. Additional data were collected through pupil interviews and analysis of teacher plans, pupil assignments, and school policies.

Findings:

1. A phenomenon of "accommodation" was noted; that is, the school and teachers willingly made efforts "to adjust the demands of school life to bring them more into correspondence with the realities of adolescent life." An example of accommodation is modifying the school and classroom demands made of pupils and helping pupils meet them. Accommodation appears to maintain, or at least does not help to improve, pupil academic disengagement. Instructional accommodations appear more commonly in regular than in special education classes. Personal accommodation by which a teacher responds to personal needs of individual students is more common in LD classes.

2. Unintended side-effects of accommodation seem to be:
   a. pupil expectation that accommodations will always be made,
   b. failure of pupils to become actively engaged with and to understand class work, and
   c. pupil boredom and apathy.

Conclusion: Accommodation may serve to keep at-risk pupils in school; however, it seems to have negative side-effects.

Study 21. Saka (1989)

Purpose: To identify factors associated with pupil achievement in reading and math.

Sample: 165 public elementary schools in Hawaii.

Method: A number of variables that other studies had found to be associated with school effectiveness were studied to see if they were associated with Hawaiian pupil achievement scores on Stanford Achievement Tests.

Findings: The following variables were significantly related to pupil success in both reading and math unless otherwise noted:

1. greater teacher experience,
2. lower percentage of pupils receiving public assistance,
3. lower percentage of special education pupils,
4. lower percentage of pupils with limited ability in English,

5. lower percentage of pupils with language needs (and reading scores), and

6. lower percentage of pupils with language needs (and math achievement)

Conclusion: The percentage of pupils in a school with language needs prior to receiving formal education, the percentage of teachers in a school with less than five years of experience, and the percentage of pupils receiving public assistance explain the most significant amounts of variation in achievement on reading and math scores.

Study 22. Yelton, Miller and Ruscoe (1989)

Purpose: To explore the relationship between school climate variables and reading and math achievement.

Sample: K-12 teachers in 88 predominantly white, rural Kentucky elementary, middle, and high schools.

Method: Data was obtained from a statewide survey that asked teacher respondents to indicate their degree of agreement with statements related to "school learning climate, teacher expectations for student achievement, and sense of efficacy." That data was correlated with school SES variables and reading and math achievement results. The strongest correlates and other factors were placed in a path mode for elementary, middle, and high school levels.

Findings include:

1. Teachers' positive expectations, or the extent to which teachers expect pupils to learn now and in the future, were highly correlated with elementary school reading and math achievement.

2. Community educational level, percentage of subsidized lunches, and instructional leadership all are significantly related to either emphasis on achievement, safe and orderly environment, or heterogeneous grouping in both elementary and middle schools.

3. Subsidized lunch has a significant relationship with teacher expectations at the elementary level.

4. In elementary schools, both emphasis on achievement and efficacy are related to teacher expectations, which in turn is highly related to math and reading achievement.

5. In high school reading and math, subsidized lunch is negatively related to emphasis on achievement and positively related to safe and orderly environment, while instructional leadership is positively related to safe and orderly environment.

36

Conclusions: The SES composition of the school affects teachers' expectations of pupil performance. In elementary schools instructional leadership seems to result in "emphasis on achievement" and does have an impact on both teacher expectations and achievement. Efficacy and expectations are causally related in some way across all levels of schooling.

Although each of the effective school investigations summarized here has somewhat different purposes, samples, and methods, there is sufficient agreement in their findings to provide some *tentative* conclusions about the characteristics of effective schools. Table 3 on pages 38 and 39 shows which studies support similar findings.

With regard to a principal's attributes contributing to effective schools, the following seem to be supported by research: fosters clear academic goals and communicates high expectations that pupils will achieve them, is deeply involved in the school's instructional program, demonstrates strong leadership and management skills, and regularly monitors what teachers and pupils are doing.

The attributes of teachers in effective schools are somewhat less clear since the school is the unit of measure. However, they seem to include holding high expectations for pupils, individualizing instruction, evaluating pupils frequently, and communicating regularly with parents. (Chapter Three will deal in greater depth with research on teacher effectiveness.) Overall, effective schools seem to have an orderly climate. Finally, when keeping pupils in school is the hoped-for result, then accommodation makes a difference.

Some Limitations of Effective Schools Research

As with most research in education, the research on effective schools has its methodological shortcomings. Some of these have been identified by, among others, Cruickshank (1986), Cuban (1983), Farrar et al. (1984), Firestone and Herriott (1982), Good and Brophy (1986), Purkey and Smith (1983), Ralph and Fennessey (1983), Rogers (1982), Rowan et al. (1983), and Stedman (1987). Following are selected criticisms.

1. When exemplary schools are nominated by others, bias is a major concern. Schools may be touted as exemplary by enthusiastic school district administrators without corroborating evidence. Some schools may be riding on past reputations but are no longer truly exceptional.

2. When schools nominated as exemplary are observed, the observation usually is for only brief periods. Thus there may not be longitudinal data showing that such schools are effective over time.

3. When schools are informed that they are to be involved in effective schools research, there is the possibility that test data used as a criterion measure might be inflated by teaching to the test.

Table 3. Comparative findings of school effectiveness research.

	Austin	Biniaminov & Glasman	Brookover & Lezotte	Brookover et al.	California	Coulson	Edmonds	Edmonds & Frederickson	Hallinger & Murphy	Harnisch	Madden et al.	Miller et al.	New York	Rutter et al. (2 studies)	Saka	Stedman	Venesky & Winfield	Weber	Wellisch et al.	Yelton et al.
Principals:																				
1. Hold clear academic goals/high expectations.	X		X	X		X		X	X		X		X				X	X	X	
2. Provide instructional leadership.	X		X			X	X	X			X		X					X	X	
3. Demonstrate strong leadership/management.	X		X			X	X	X			X								X	
4. Regularly monitor staff and students.								X												
5. Positive interactions with teachers.																				
Teachers:																				
1. Maintain good communication with the principal.														X						X
2. Hold high expectations.		X																		
3. Have fewer years of teaching experience.															X					
4. Have more years of teaching experience.																				
School or Classroom Climate:																				
1. Is orderly and conducive to learning.				X			X	X		X	X		X	X		X		X		
2. Promotes students' feelings of efficacy.	X			X						X	X					X				
3. Emphasizes cognitive goals.										X				X						
4. Provides for student responsibility in school affairs.																				
5. Maintains high expectations.				X												X		X		
6. Is accepting and supportive.																X				
7. Promotes diversity.																				
8. Promotes a common sense of purpose among faculty and staff.					X													X		

38

Curriculum:
1. Staff frequently interact and review the curriculum.
2. Curriculum is coherent and coordinated.
3. Schools use different but single basal series.
4. Reading is emphasized.
5. Student development is emphasized.
6. There is integration among subjects.
7. Teacher-developed remedial programs are used.
8. Students visit the library weekly.

Instruction:
1. Is individualized.
2. Is coordinated grade and school wide.
3. Includes frequent homework.
4. Utilizes preventive policies and techniques.
5. Makes use of reinforcement rather than punishments.
6. Maximizes instructional time.
7. Includes diagnostic approaches.
8. Is supported by librarians.
9. Includes oral and written book reports.
10. Includes reinstruction when needed.
11. Is the responsibility of staff and they are held accountable.
12. Utilizes student logs.
13. Frequently makes use of supplementary materials.
14. Uses phonics.
15. Emphasizes whole class techniques.

Evaluation:
1. Students are frequently evaluated.
2. Classrooms/teachers are regularly observed.

Special or Extra Staffing:

Other:
1. Open communication with parents is maintained.
2. Inservice and faculty meetings are frequent and productive.
3. Willingness of school and teachers to make compromises for pupils.

4. Schools are often designated as effective based on a single outcome measure (usually scores on standardized tests), and they tend to score high on that measure. The same schools might not be judged effective if other outcome measures are used. The National Center for Educational Statistics provides 54 alternative outcome measures that, in addition to test scores, includes Carnegie units earned, graduation rate, pupil-teacher ratio, class size, teacher abilities, and pupil attendance, among others (ASCD Update, January 1985). Cohen (1988) likewise offers a choice of alternative outcome measures including teenage pregnancy rates, dropout rates, employer satisfaction, and parent involvement. (See Study 20 above for a description of the investigation of a school with lower than expected dropout rate.)

5. Sometimes the most common variables or outcomes measured are not well defined operationally. A practitioner or another researcher may not be clear as to what investigators mean by "clear academic goals, high expectations, strong leadership, or orderly climate." Thus when trying to draw some implications from the findings of research for a school, or when designing further inquiry, we may be at a loss as to how to proceed. Relatedly, different researchers choose to observe different aspects of schooling. Thus all potentially promising effectiveness variables are studied in different amount and degree, and some surely have not been subjected to investigation as yet.

6. Another limitation is that only a small sample of schools has been studied overall, and most studies are conducted in low SES schools located in urban communities.

7. When data are aggregated at the school or district level, we do not know what variables are most influential at different grade levels, in different subject areas, or with different pupil subpopulations. Thus it becomes difficult to generalize from effective schools research.

Given these limitations, the findings of effective schools research must be viewed tentatively. Nevertheless, for the most part these studies confirm what we share as professional wisdom. Therefore, they have value for teachers and teacher educators.

How Effective Schools Research
Informs Teaching and Teacher Education

Given the inquiry models of teaching and teacher education presented in Chapter One, one can conceive of several ways that effective schools research can serve to inform preservice and inservice education. Most obviously, it has implications for teaching and school practice, for the teacher preparation curriculum, and for teacher educator preparation.

Clearly, both preservice and inservice teachers should be aware of the individual studies and the tentative aggregated findings. Teachers can profit from reflecting on research done in schools similar to their own. For example, inner-city, elementary teachers could profit substantially from the studies of Weber, Klitgaard and Hall, New York Office of Education Performance Review, Madden et al., Edmonds and Frederickson, and others. On the basis of these studies, several school districts and state education agencies already have undertaken school improvement programs with moderate success (Stedman 1987). In addition, some staff developers have designed frameworks for thinking about the relative importance of the variables operating in identified effective schools (Murphy et al. 1985).

For students in preservice programs, these studies provide insights into characteristics of schools and instructional practices that will be helpful in their future work. Among other things, preservice students will become aware that schools increasingly are being held accountable. Moreover, they will learn what schools are being held accountable for and how accountability is determined. They will become familiar with the current knowledge base of what constitutes effective schooling and also the limitations of such knowledge. With this knowledge, they can begin to reflect on how it might be transformed into school practice. For example: How can schools and teachers help pupils to master basic skills? How can clear school and academic missions be established and maintained? How can strong instructional leadership be supported? How can pupil progress be frequently monitored? How can positive school climate be established? Knowledge of the effective schools research and reflecting on it using the above questions should help make preservice students more thoughtful and prudent in making decisions as they enter the profession.

Sadly, the research on effective schools seldom is addressed in the preparation of teacher educators. No mandates exist that teacher preparers study what constitutes effective schooling, however defined. Moreover, little consensus exists about what the knowledge base should be for those who prepare our teachers. Mostly we presume that completion of the doctorate in any area of education is sufficient. But without a solid knowledge base, it is doubtful that teacher preparers can do more than share their personal experience and ideology (Dunkin and Biddle 1974). *Teacher educators need to know what is known in order to prepare others to work effectively in the schools.*

Even though the knowledge base accumulated to date is fragmentary and incomplete, and even though much more needs to be known about the phenomenon of schooling, enough is known and should be used to guide policy and practice in schools and teacher education institutions. The challenge, then, is to infuse this knowledge into the curriculum of both teachers and teacher preparers. Being informed about effective schools research permits us to reflect on it, to scrutinize how it is conducted and whether it is valid, and finally to ask ourselves how it may serve us better.

References

Austin, G. "Exemplary Schools and the Search for Effectiveness." *Educational Leadership* 37, no. 1 (1979): 10-14.

Austin G. *Progress Evaluation: A Comprehensive Study of Outliers*. College Park: Center for Educational Research and Development and the Maryland State Department of Education, February 1978. ERIC No. 160 644

Biniaminov, I., and Glasman, N. "School Determinants of Student Achievement in Secondary Education." *American Educational Research Journal* 20, no. 2 (1983): 251-68.

Bracey, G.W. "SES Talks, Money Walks." *Phi Delta Kappan* 69 (January 1988): 376-77.

Brookover, W., and Lezotte, L. "Changes in School Chracteristics Coincident with Changes in Student Achievement." East Lansing: Michigan State University Institute for Research on Teaching, 1979. ERIC No. 181 005

Brookover, W.; Beady, C.; Flood, P.; Schweitzer, J.; and Wisenbaker, J. *School Social Systems and Student Achievement: Schools Can Make a Difference*. New York: Praeger, 1979.

Bureau of Educational Personnel Development. *Do Teachers Make a Difference? A Report on Recent Research on Pupil Achievement*. Washington, D.C.: Department of Health, Education and Welfare, 1970.

California Assembly Office of Research. "California Study Assesses Factors in School Effectiveness." *Education Week*, 11 April 1984.

Cohen, M. "Designing State Assessment Systems." *Phi Delta Kappan* 69 (April 1988): 583-88.

Coulson, J. *Overview of the National Evaluation of the Emergency School Aid Act*. Santa Monica, Calif.: System Development, July 1977.

Cruickshank, D. "A Synopsis of Effective Schools Research: Why Is It Done? How Is It Done? What Are Its Findings? How Are They Implemented?" *Illinois School Research & Development* 22, no. 3 (1986): 112-27.

Cuban, L. "Effective Schools: A Friendly But Cautionary Note." *Phi Delta Kappan* 64 (June 1983): 695-96.

Dunkin, M.J., and Biddle, B.J. *The Study of Teaching*. New York: Holt, Rinehart and Winston, 1974.

Edmonds, R. "Effective Schools for the Urban Poor." *Educational Leadership* 37, no. 1 (1979): 15-27.

Edmonds, R., and Frederickson, N. *Search for Effective Schools: The Identification and Analysis of City Schools that Are Instructionally Effective for Poor Children*. Cambridge, Mass.: Harvard University Center for Policy Studies, 1978.

Farrar, E.; Nenfela, B.; and Miles, M. "Effective Schools Programs in High Schools: Social Promotion or Movement by Merit." *Phi Delta Kappan* 65 (June 1984): 701-706.

Firestone, W., and Herriott, R. "Prescriptions for Effective Elementary Schools Don't Fit Secondary Schools." *Educational Leadership* 40 (December 1982): 31-33.

Good, T., and Brophy, J. "School Effects." In *Handbook of Research on Teaching*, edited by M. Wittrock. New York: Macmillan, 1986.

Hallinger, P., and Murphy, J. "Characteristics of Highly Effective Elementary School Reading Programs." *Educational Leadership* 42 (February 1985): 39-42.

Harnisch, D. "An Investigation of Factors Associated with Effective Public High Schools." Paper presented at the annual meeting of the Mid-Western Educational Research Association in Chicago, 1985.

Jencks, C., et al. *Inequality: A Reassessment of the Effect of Family and Schooling in America*. New York: Basic Books, 1972.

Kean, M., et al. *What Works in Reading?* Philadelphia: Philadelphia School District, May 1979.

Klitgaard, R., and Hall, G. "Are There Unusually Effective Schools?" *Journal of Human Resources* 74 (1974): 90-106.

Madden, J., et al. *School Effectiveness Study: State of California*. Sacramento: California Department of Education, 1976.

Miller, S.; Leinhardt, G.; and Zigmond, N. "Influencing Engagement Through Accommodation: An Ethnographic Study of At-Risk Students." *American Educational Research Association Journal* 25 (Winter 1988): 465-87.

Murphy, J.; Weil, M.; Hallinger, O.; and Mitman, A. "School Effectiveness: A Conceptual Framework." *Educational Forum* 49 (Spring 1985): 361-74.

New York State Office of Education Performance Review. *School Factors Influencing Reading Achievement: A Case Study of Two Inner-City Schools*. Albany, March 1974. ERIC No. 089 211

Purkey, S., and Smith, M. "Effective Schools: A Review." *Elementary School Journal* 83 (March 1983): 427-52.

Ralph, J., and Fennessey, J. "Science or Reform: Some Questions About the Effective Schools Model." *Phi Delta Kappan* 64 (June 1983): 689-94.

"Rogers Questions 'Effective Schools'." *ASCD Update* (May 1982).

Rowan, B.; Bossert, S.T.; and Dwyer, D.C. "Research on Effective Schools: A Cautionary Note." *Educational Researcher* 12, no. 4 (1983): 24-31.

Rutter, M.; Maugham, B.; Mortimore, P.; Ouston, J.; and Smith, A. *Fifteen Thousand Hours: Secondary Schools and Their Effects on Children*. Cambridge, Mass.: Harvard University Press, May 1979.

Saka, T. "Indicators of School Effectiveness: Which Are the Most Valid and What Impacts upon Them?" Paper presented at the annual meeting of the American Educational Research Association in San Francisco, March 1989.

Stedman, L. "It's Time to Change the School Effectiveness Formula." *Phi Delta Kappan* 69 (November 1987): 215-24.

"Top State Education Officials Support Indicators: Results Could Be National Tests and State-by-State Comparisons." *ASCD Update* (January 1985): 1, 6, 7.

U.S. Department of Health, Education and Welfare. *Equality of Educational Opportunity: Summary Report.* (The Coleman Report). Washington, D.C.: U.S. Government Printing Office, 1966.

Venesky, R., and Winfield, L. *Schools that Succeed Beyond Expectations in Reading.* Studies on Education Technical Report No. 1. Newark: University of Delaware, 1979. ERIC No. 177 484

Walberg, H., and Fowler, W. "Expenditure and Size Efficiency of Public School Districts." *Educational Researcher* 16 (October 1987): 5-13.

Weber, G. *Inner-City Children Can Be Taught to Read: Four Successful Schools.* CBE Occasional Paper No. 18. Washington, D.C.: Council for Basic Education, 1971.

Wellisch, J., et al. "School Management and Organization in Successful Schools." *Sociology of Education* no. 5 (1978): 211-26.

Yelton, B.; Miller, S.; and Ruscoe G. "Path Analysis of Correlates of School Effectiveness: Model Comparison Across Elementary, Middle, and High School." Paper presented at the annual meeting of the American Educational Research Association in San Francisco, March 1989.

3 The Search for Knowledge About Effective Educational Practices

There long has been a keen interest in identifying specific curricular and instructional practices that are effective in accomplishing school goals. The reasons for this interest are many. To begin with, education is a vast enterprise. However, it must be more than big business; it must be good business. If students spend more than 12,000 hours in formal education before graduating from high school, that time should be well spent. Doubts arise about whether that time is spent well when, for example, comparative studies of mathematics achievement in 14 industrialized nations rank U.S. eighth-graders in 12th place (Stevenson 1983). A second reason is that the citizens expect schools to use the most effective means to prepare the next generation to contribute to the nation's social and economic well-being. The most important reason of all is that our children deserve to have the most effective educational practices in order to gain the knowlege, skills, and attitudes that will serve them now and throughout their lives.

Efforts to Aggregate Research on Effective Educational Practices

Over the past four decades, there have been several efforts to identify specific, effective educational practices, K-12. In the 1950s the National Education Association began its popular *What Research Says to the Teacher* series (NEA 1954-67). These concise booklets summarized research on a variety of topics of direct interest to teachers. The series included titles on the teaching of reading, arithmetic, spelling, and handwriting; reporting pupil progress; homework; science instruction; classroom organization; group processes; and many others.

In 1961 two well-received compilations of educational practice were Brickell's *Commissioner's Catalog of Educational Change* (1961) and Trump and Baynham's *Guide to Better Schools* (1961). The Brickell work was a post-

Sputnik survey of schools in New York State designed to document the extent to which new practices were being used. He reported that many changes had been made in the teaching of foreign languages, science, mathematics, English, and social studies but noted that "very few of the programs had been adequately evaluated" (p. 29). Among the specific educational practices that were being used were: individualization, non-graded classroom organization, Cuisenaire rods, television, team teaching, programmed spelling, house plans, flexible grouping, new math, new science, honors programs, language development, dual progress, early foreign language, summer enrichment, Saturday seminars, acceleration, advanced placement courses, teacher aides, non-Western studies, Joplin Plan, Great Books, lay readers for evaluating student writing, and outdoor education.

The Trump and Baynham publication, *Guide to Better Schools*, is a call for change advocating such practices as independent study, use of inquiry learning, use of discussion, human relations training, team teaching, use of teacher assistants, and flexible scheduling of classes.

In *School Curriculum Reform* (1964), Goodlad described a variety of innovative educational practices instituted to improve K-12 course offerings in such subject fields as mathematics, physics, biology, chemistry, elementary school science, social sciences, English, and modern foreign languages. Many of the practices reported were from the federally funded curriculum development projects of the late Fifties and early Sixties: University of Illinois Committee on School Mathematics, School Mathematics Study Group, Physical Science Study Committee, Biological Sciences Curriculum Study, Chemical Bond Approach Project, Elementary School Science Project, High School Geography Project, and the English Composition Project.

Unruh and Alexander (1970) enumerate other "innovative" practices in secondary education including individualized instruction, independent study, student-planned forums, out-of-school-time projects, human relations workshops, team learning, independent study, travel-study, work-study, community study, aesthetic education, school-within-a-school, multiple tracking, year-round schooling, differentiated staffing, programmed instruction, simulation and gaming, and educational television.

Callahan and Clark (1977) added to the list of promising educational practices with computers, education vouchers, desegregation, and mini-courses. Two rich sources of data on educational practices indicating continuing interest in this topic are the four-volume *Encyclopedia of Educational Research* (Mitzel 1982) and the *Handbook of Research on Teaching* (Wittrock 1986).

The sources cited above by no means provide an exhaustive list of educational practices of interest to teachers and teacher educators. Suffice it to say, there are many educational practices, so many in fact that it can be confusing to teachers and teacher educators as to which to use or to recommend. There are almost limitless possibilities for practices relating to what to teach, how to teach, how to organize the curriculum, what materials and technology to use and how to use them, how to organize pupils for instruction, how to organize the school, how to report pupils' progress, how to allocate staff, and so on.

What Educational Practices Are Validated by Research?

Many of the reported K-12 educational practices are touted as useful, innovative, even exciting. They are *presumed* to be beneficial, but are they? In recent years several researchers have conducted studies to determine the actual or observed effectiveness of a variety of education practices (Walberg 1984; Ellson 1986; U.S. Department of Education 1986; Slavin 1987; Slavin and Madden 1989). The rest of this chapter is devoted to a review of these reseachers' work as they addressed the question, "What is an effective educational practice?" The reader should keep in mind that each of them uses a somewhat different definition and approach in addressing the question.

Walberg (1984)

Walberg begins by positing a "theory of educational productivity." It goes something like this: Traditionally, the expected outcomes of education and schooling are either affective, behavioral, or cognitive learning. The researcher's task is to determine what variables or factors have "causal influences on pupil learning." Walberg identifies nine factors that fall into three larger clusters as follows:

1. *Student aptitude* including a) ability and prior achievement as measured by standardized tests, b) developmental stage (chronological age or level of maturation), and c) motivation and self-concept;
2. *Instruction* including a) amount of time pupils engage in learning and b) quality of the instructional experience; and
3. *Environment* including a) home, b) classroom social group, c) peer group outside of school, and d) use of out-of-school time, specifically leisure television viewing.

Using this model, Walberg and his colleagues synthesized nearly 3,000 pieces of research that bore on the three clusters and nine factors subsumed therein, conducted case studies of Japanese and American classrooms, and analyzed three large statistical data sets (National Assessment of Educational Progress, High School and Beyond, and the International Study of Educational Achievement). Several different kinds of findings are presented below.

According to the investigators, the three clusters of nine factors are each and all "powerful and consistent in influencing learning" (p. 22). However, some of the factors may substitute for others. "[I]mmense quantities of time may be required for a moderate amount of learning if motivation, ability, or instructional quality is minimal" (p. 22). Moreover, Walberg feels many of these factors can be influenced; that is, they are alterable by teachers and/or parents.

> For example, the 12 years of 180 six-hour days in elementary and secondary schools add up to only about 13 percent of waking, potentially productive, time during their first 18 years of life. If a large fraction of the student's waking time normally under the control of parents . . . were to be spent in academically stimulating conditions in the home and in the peer group, then the total amount of the student's total learning time would be dramatically raised beyond the 13 percent. (p. 22)

Of particular interest here are Walberg's conclusions with regard to the effects of various aspects and methods of instruction. Table 4 depicts the relationships he found between various instructional practices and learning stated in terms of tenths of standard deviations. According to Slavin (1987, p. 112), an effect size of 1.0 would indicate that pupils in the treatment groups gained one standard deviation more on the criterion measure than did pupils in control groups. Typically, this is equivalent to gaining one or two grade-level equivalents.

Several things are worthy of comment. First, some of the "effect" sizes are quite large. Prominent is the use of "reinforcement" for correct performance. Walberg notes that in studies in which use of reinforcement is compared with its non-use, the mean difference between the experimental and control groups is an average of 1.17 standard deviations. This means that when pupils who are provided with reinforcement are compared with pupils who are not, the pupils differ markedly, with the mean performance of reinforced learners being more than a full standard deviation higher on the performance measure (for example, arithmetic). That is a whopping difference! Another practice with large instructional effects (.97) is the use of "cues and feedback," which also are supported by what we know from the psychology of learning.

Additionally, large instructional effects are associated with "acceleration" (1.0), that is, providing advanced work for K-12 pupils with high intellectual aptitude and outstanding test scores; and with "reading training" (.97). The latter involves coaching in such skills as adjusting reading speeds, skimming, and finding answers to specific questions.

Since normal effect sizes are around .20, a number of Walberg's findings point to promising practices that teachers and teacher educators should

Table 4. Relationship of educational practices to pupil learning.

Method	Effect
Reinforcement	1.17
Acceleration	1.00
Reading Training	.97
Cues and Feedback	.97
Science Mastery Learning	.81
Cooperative Learning	.76
Reading Experiment	.60
Personalized Instruction	.57
Adaptive Instruction	.45
Tutoring	.40
Instructional Time	.38
Individualized Science	.35
Higher-Order Questions	.34
Diagnostic Prescriptive Methods	.33
Individualized Instruction	.32
Individualized Mathematics	.32
New Science Curricula	.31
Teacher Expectations	.28
Computer Assisted Instruction	.24
Sequenced Lessons	.24
Advance Organizers	.23
New Mathematics Curricula	.18
Inquiry Biology	.16
Homogeneous Groups	.10
Class Size	.09
Programmed Instruction	− .03
Mainstreaming	− .12

know about and be skilled in using. These include: cooperative learning in small groups, mastery learning, personalized instruction, and tutoring.

Moderate to small effects on instruction are associated with certain post-Sputnik science and mathematics curricula, with higher teacher expectations (confirming effective schools research reviewed in Chapter Two), and with the use of advanced organizers (relating material to be learned to that which already has been learned).

On the other hand, Walberg found no support in the studies he reviewed on educational practices related to academic learning for reduced class size, programmed instruction, and mainstreaming. Also of interest are Walberg's conclusions with regard to the effects of environmental factors (home, classroom, peer group, and television viewing). These factors may also be amenable to alteration to some extent. Table 5 lists the effects of environmental factors on pupil learning.

Table 5. Relationship of environmental factors to pupil learning.

Method	Effect
Graded Homework	.79
Class Morale	.60
Home Interventions	.50
Home Environment	.37
Assigned Homework	.28
Socioeconomic Status	.25
Peer Group	.24
Television	−.05

Once more, there are practices that would seem to be most promising, particularly "homework" (.79) that is graded or commented upon, "class morale" (.60) perceived by pupils as high, and "home interventions" (.50) that are intended to improve pupil learning in the home (parent-child discussions about school assignments), and time for leisure reading and reduced television viewing (-.05).

Ellson (1986)

Our second research reviewer, Ellson, defines an effective educational practice as one that satisfies the relative production ratio of 2.0 or more; that is, when two educational practices are compared, one must be 100% or more better than the other in achieving one of three teacher productivity indices: teacher effectiveness, cost efficiency, or cost effectiveness.

Ellson's approach was to identify 75 research studies, "largely ignored, that report great differences in one or more of the three indices of teaching productivity." Ellson found 125 educational practices that met the 2.0 criterion.

He grouped them into two categories reflecting somewhat different characteristics. The first category is *conventional teaching* with four variants: 1) augmented conventional teaching, 2) conventional tutoring and conventional tutoring as a supplement to conventional teaching, 3) content modification in conventional teaching, and 4) procedural modification of conventional teaching. The second category is *nonconventional teaching* with three variants: 1) programmed learning, 2) programmed teaching, and 3) performance-based instruction and design.

Conventional teaching is defined as teaching procedures generally acceptable and in common use that are teacher-centered; that is, the teacher or tutor is almost entirely responsible for how the teaching is done and to a lesser extent is responsible for choosing the curricular materials or deciding what will be taught.

Augmented conventional teaching occurs when conventional teaching is supplemented by additional resources. These might include special equipment and materials; personnel or funds to make the work of teachers easier (for example, by hiring teacher aides to perform non-instructional tasks thus making more time available for instruction and individualization); reducing class size or the teacher-pupil ratio; modifying content; and increasing morale, salaries, and the quality and qualifications of the teacher force. Educational practices that exemplify augmented conventional teaching include: the College-Bound Project Method, the Fernald Method, R-3 Program, Montessori Method, Enriched Curriculum, Diagnostically Based Curriculum and Success Environment (see Ellson, pages 113-114, for descriptions). These practices, among other things, require smaller classes, make extra time available for instruction, and make use of aides, individualization, and a wide range of teaching materials.

Results of studies of augmented conventional teaching suggest that if funds are available for implementing such practices, the results would, among other things, increase I.Q. scores, reduce classroom disruptions, increase grade-level scores on tests of reading and arithmetic, and improve scores on pupil tests of anxiety.

Tutoring, as defined by Ellson, occurs when non-professionally trained instructors, including students working under a teacher's direction, improvise teaching and sometimes improvise materials. Educational practices exemplifying tutoring include: Youth Teaches Youth Program, Morgan and Toy's work, and the work of Deutsch (see Ellison, page 115, for descriptions).

Results of the use of tutoring suggest benefits in the form of improved pupil reading, spelling, and arithmetic as well as benefits for the tutors themselves.

Content modification in conventional teaching is essentially conventional teaching wherein the curriculum is reorganized or varied in some special way to give it a different emphasis. However, instruction is still conventional in that it is teacher-centered. Examples of this category of educational practice include: substituting the International Teaching Alphabet for the standard one, using the Algorithmization Technique for teaching Russian grammar, using the Language Stimulation Method, and using "sight" word instead of phonics in teaching reading (see Ellson, page 115, for descriptions).

Results of studies reveal that use of the Algorithmization Technique was productive and that use of Language Stimulation was associated with pupil gains in both I.Q. and psycholinguistic ability.

Procedural modification of conventional teaching occurs when a relatively simple modification occurs in a teacher's skill, practice, or outlook. Examples given include Rosenthal's "Pygmalion effect," whereby a teacher's optimistic outlook and expectation of learner success results in greater pupil achievement, and the Community Integrated Procedure, wherein the placement of disadvantaged children in socioeconomically integrated classes results in enhanced language performance.

Ellson also placed some of the 75 "neglected" research studies in the "nonconventional teaching" cluster with its three variations: programmed learning, programmed teaching, and performance-based instruction and design. In this cluster, detailed decisions, dealing for the most part with what and how to teach, are made by instructional systems designers who write the curriculum and the instructional program. In these variations instruction is program-centered, and teachers must follow detailed prescriptions.

The first variation, *programmed learning*, is defined as self-instruction whereby the pupil interacts with materials in a predetermined, detailed way. The subject matter to be learned is reduced to small bits of information, and positive reinforcement is commonly offered as each bit of information is successfully learned. This variation has characteristics similar to the conventional recitation method in that it employs questions, answers, praise, or relearning. Programmed learning is the major means of instruction in most extension or distance education programs and is the method of choice in Britain's Open University, where students appear to learn as well as students who are conventionally taught; yet the costs are one-third of those for conventional instruction.

Programmed teaching, the second variation, includes group instruction and tutoring in which teachers or tutors follow a tightly structured program and script. The prerequisite knowledge is covered in the teaching materials. So-called "teacher-proof" programmed teaching assumes that if the program is followed explicitly, then learning is maximized. Educational practices assigned to this variation include: the Bell System First-Aid and Personal Safety Course, Telepac Programs, Peer-Mediated Instruction Techniques, and perhaps most familiar, Bereiter and Englemann's Direct Instruction Method (descriptions are found in Ellson, page 118). Evaluations of the use of these instructional methods support their superiority by such measures as gains in mean scores and reduction in the time required to learn the criterion content.

Ellson's third variation of nonconventional teaching is *performance-based instruction and design*, in which instructional objectives are carefully specified and instruction is geared to achieving those objectives. Learning is monitored constantly, and instruction is altered if necessary in order to achieve the objectives more efficiently. Revision and refinement are ongoing. Ellson's examples include 16 reported by Taylor dealing with military training curricula, Sherrill's Military Court Reporting, and Meleragno's Early Reading (descriptions are found in Ellson, pages 120-21). Evaluations of these methods of instruction report relative production ratios of more than 2.0 for most of them.

Overall, Ellson notes that in only 26% of the studies comparing conventional with nonconventional teaching practices did the conventional demonstrate superiority either in terms of teacher effectiveness, cost efficiency, or cost effectiveness. He leaves us with the question, "Why are we not teaching as well and as economically as the state of the art or technology permits?"

Slavin (1987)

Slavin and his associates have evaluated practices used in school districts to improve the achievement of students at risk of school failure. According to Slavin: "With few exceptions, the programs we located that presented consistent and convincing evidence of instructional effectiveness look completely different from traditional . . . Chapter 1 models" (p. 111). (Chapter 1 refers to those federally sponsored programs intended to help academically at-risk students from falling behind.) In general, the most effective programs are those that are designed so that teachers can meet a wide range of pupil needs. They include "continuous-progress programs" and "cooperative learning programs."

Continuous-progress programs enable pupils to proceed at their own pace through a series of well-defined objectives. Pupils at similar levels of achievement are taught in small groups. Regrouping is frequent, even across grade levels. The programs cited for convincing evidence of instructional effectiveness are: DISTAR (grades K-6 reading and math), U-SAIL (grades 1-9 reading and math), PEGASUS-PACE (grades K-8 reading), Project INSTRUCT (grades K-3 reading), GEMS (grades K-12 reading), and Early Childhood Preventative Curriculum (grade 1 reading).

Cooperative learning programs involve a small group of heterogeneous students organized as a learning team. The students work together and receive recognition based on their team effort. Similar to continuous-progress programs, the pupils proceed at their own rates in "skill-based subgroups." Programs cited of this sort are: Team Accelerated Instruction (grades 3-6 math) and Cooperative Integrated Reading and Composition (grades 3-5 reading and writing).

Another category of effective instructional practices Slavin calls "intensive supplementary models." These offer high quality instruction for relatively short periods and usually supplement regular classroom instruction. Included in this category are preventive tutoring, remedial tutoring, and computer-assisted instruction. Preventive tutoring uses specially trained adults to work one-on-one with, for example, at-risk, first-grade pupils. Remedial tutoring uses adult volunteers or older students to work with pupils needing remedial help in basic skills. Computer-assisted instruction uses time with a computer program, normally for additional drill and practice in reading and math.

Programs cited in the three subsets of the intensive supplementary category are: preventive tutoring programs, including Programmed Tutorial Reading (grade 1 reading), Prevention of Learning Disabilities (grades 1-2 reading), Wallach Tutorial Program (grade 1 reading), and Reading Recovery (grade 1 reading); remedial tutoring programs, including Training for Turnabout Volunteers (tutors from grades 7-9, pupils in grades 1-6 reading and math), School Volunteer Development Project (grades 2-6 reading and math), and Success Controlled Optimal Reading Experience (grades 1-6 reading and math); and computer-assisted instruction programs, including Computer Curriculum Corp. Study 1 (grades 1-6 math, 3-6 reading and language), Computer Curriculum Corp. Study 2 (grades 3-6 math), Computer Curriculum Corp. Study 3 (2-9 reading), and Basic Literacy Through Microcomputers (grades 1-3 reading). Clearly, the large number of nonconventional teaching programs cited as effective would seem to support and strengthen the findings of Ellson (1986) and Slavin and Madden (1989).

Slavin and Madden (1989)

For programs in elementary reading and mathematics to be considered effective, Slavin and Madden state that they must meet three criteria:

1. The program could be replicated in other schools.
2. The program had to have been evaluated for a semester or more and had to have been compared to a control group or to have shown convincing evidence of year-to-year gains.
3. The program had to provide effects of at least one-quarter of a standard deviation difference to be considered educationally as well as statistically significant (pp. 5-6).

Programs meeting these criteria were organized into three categories: prevention, classroom change, and remediation. Prevention programs tended to be for preschool, kindergarten, and first grade and provided intensive

54

instruction early in order to prevent the need for later remediation. Kindergarten programs making the cut include: Alpha Phonics, Astra's Magic Math, MECCA, TALK, MARC, and PLAY. First-grade programs cited are Programmed Tutorial Reading, Prevention of Learning Disabilities-New York, Wallach Tutorial Program, Reading Recovery, and Early Childhood Prevention Curriculum. Slavin and Madden did note that such programs tended to have more immediate than lasting effects on pupils, that is, the effects diminish until by the second or third grade they wash out.

The classroom change category is comprised of "instructional methods with a demonstrated capacity to accelerate student achievement, especially that of pupils at-risk." It includes continuous-progress programs and cooperative learning. Effective continuous-progress programs include most of those cited in Slavin's 1987 findings: DISTAR, U-SAIL, PEGASUS-PACE, Project INSTRUCT, and GEMS. An additional one is ECRI (grades K-3 reading). Effective cooperative learning programs cited here and also in Slavin's 1987 review include Team Accelerated Instruction and Cooperative Integrated Reading and Composition. Additional ones cited in Slavin and Madden (1989) are Student Teams-Achievement Divisions (grades 3-5 math) and Companion Reading (grade 1 reading).

Remediation (supplementary/remedial) programs are those most often used with pupils who are behind in basic skills. They include remedial tutoring programs and computer-assisted instruction. Effective tutoring programs include those cited by Slavin (1987): Training for Turnabout Volunteer, School Volunteer Development Project, and Success Controlled Optimal Reading Experience. Effective computer-assisted programs also cited in Slavin's (1987) review include Computer Curriculum Corp. and Basic Literacy Through Microcomputer. Additional ones are Los Angeles Unified School District (grades 1-6 math, grades 3-6 reading, language), Lafayette Parish Title 1 (grades 3-6 math), and Merrimack Education Center (grades 2-9 reading).

Slavin and Madden conclude that there are general principles that characterize effective educational programs for pupils at risk. They are comprehensive and include manuals, curriculum materials, and lesson guides. Effective preventive and remedial programs are intensive, using one-on-one tutoring or individually adapted computer-assisted instruction. Effective programs frequently monitor pupil gains and modify instruction and grouping arrangements to meet individual needs.

What Works (1986)

A fourth effort to identify promising educational practices is found in a report issued by the U.S. Department of Education, titled *What Works:*

Research About Teaching and Learning (1986). In this report, effective educational practice is based on "knowledge drawn from contemporary research and from opinions of distinguished thinkers of earlier times." In the case of opinion, there must be professional consensus for a practice to be considered effective.

Essentially *What Works* enumerates 41 "findings" about how best to teach and to improve learning. The findings are grouped under three headings: home, classroom, and school. Each finding is presented on a separate page, commented on, and references supporting it are provided. An example of a finding reported from *What Works* appears as Table 6.

Table 6. Example of a finding from *What Works* (1986, p. 36).

Tutoring

Research Finding:	Students tutoring other students can lead to improved academic achievement for both student and tutor, and to positive attitudes toward coursework.
Comment:	Tutoring programs consistently raise the achievement of both the students receiving instruction and those providing it. Peer tutoring, when used as a supplement to regular classroom teaching, helps slow and underachieving students master their lessons and succeed in school. Preparing and giving the lessons also benefits the tutors themselves because they learn more about the material they are teaching.

Of the tutoring programs that have been studied, the most effective include the following elements:

- highly structured and well-planned curricula and instructional methods,
- instruction in basic content and skills (grades 1-3), especially in arithmetic, and
- a relatively short duration of instruction (a few weeks or months).

When these features were combined in the same program, the students being tutored not only learned more than they did without tutoring, they also developed a more positive attitude about what they were studying. Their tutors also learned more than students who did not tutor.

References:	Cohen, P.A., Kulik, J. A., and Kulik, C-L. C. (Summer 1982). "Educational Outcomes of Tutoring: A Meta-Analysis of Findings." *American Educational Research Journal*, Vol. 19, No. 2, pp. 237-248.

Devin-Sheehan, L., Feldman, R.S., and Allen, V.L. (1976). "Research on Children Tutoring Children: A Critical Review." *Review of Educational Research*, Vol. 46, No. 3, pp. 355-385.

Mohan, M. (1972). *Peer Tutoring as a Technique for Teaching the Unmotivated.* Fredonia, NY: State University of New York Teacher Education Research Center. ERIC Document No. ED 061154.

Rosenshine, B., and Furst, N. (1969) *The Effects of Tutoring Upon Pupil Achievement: A Research Review.* Washington, DC: U.S. Department of Education. ERIC Document No. ED 064462.

The 41 findings from *What Works* (1986) are listed below in the three aforementioned categories: home, classroom, and schools. The reader is directed to the original report for detailed descriptions and supporting references.

Home:

1. Curriculum of the home. Parents are their children's first and most influential teachers. What parents do to help their children learn is more important to academic success than how well-off the family is.

2. Reading to children. The best way for parents to help their children become better readers is to read to them even when they are very young. Children benefit most from reading aloud when they discuss stories, learn to identify letters and words, and talk about the meaning of words.

3. Independent reading. Children improve their reading ability by reading a lot. Reading achievement is directly related to the amount of reading children do in school and outside.

4. Counting. A good way to teach children simple arithmetic is to build on their informal knowledge. This is why learning to count everyday objects is an effective basis for early arithmetic lessons.

5. Early writing. Children who are encouraged to draw and scribble "stories" at an early age will later learn to compose more easily, more effectively, and with greater confidence than children who do not have this encouragement.

6. Speaking and listening. A good foundation in speaking and listening helps children become better readers.

7. Developing talent. Many highly successful individuals have above-average but not extraordinary intelligence. Accomplishment in a particular activity is often more dependent on hard work and self-discipline than on innate ability.

8. Ideals. Belief in the value of hard work, the importance of personal responsibility, and the importance of education itself contribute to greater success in school.

Classroom:

9. Getting parents involved. Parental involvement helps children learn more effectively. Teachers who are successful at involving parents in their children's schoolwork are successful because they work at it.

10. Phonics. Children get a better start in reading if they are taught phonics. Learning phonics helps them to understand the relationship between letters and sounds and to "break the code" that links the words they hear with the words they see in print.

11. Reading comprehension. Children get more out of a reading assignment when the teacher precedes the lesson with background information and follows it with discussion.

12. Science experiments. Children learn science best when they are able to do experiments so they can witness "science in action."

13. Storytelling. Telling young children stories can motivate them to read. Storytelling also introduces them to cultural values and literary traditions before they can read, write, and talk about stories by themselves.

14. Teaching writing. The most effective way to teach writing is to teach it as a process of brainstorming, composing, revising, and editing.

15. Learning mathematics. Children in early grades learn mathematics more effectively when they use physical objects in their lessons.

16. Estimating. Although students need to learn how to find exact answers to arithmetic problems, good math students also learn the skill of estimating answers. This skill can be taught.

17. Teacher expectations. Teachers who set and communicate high expectations to all their students obtain greater academic performance from those students than teachers who set low expectations.

18. Student ability and effort. Children's understanding of the relationship between being smart and hard work changes as they grow older.

19. Managing classroom time. How much time students are actively engaged in learning contributes strongly to their achievement. The amount of time available for learning is determined by the instructional and management skills of the teacher and the priorities set by the school administration.

20. Direct instruction. When teachers explain exactly what students are expected to learn, and demonstrate the steps needed to accomplish a particular academic task, students learn more.

21. Tutoring. Students tutoring other students can lead to improved academic achievement for student and tutor, and to positive attitudes toward coursework.

22. Memorization. Memorizing can help students absorb and retain the factual information on which understanding and critical thought are based.

23. Questioning. Student achievement rises when teachers ask questions that require students to apply, analyze, synthesize, and evaluate information in addition to simply recalling facts.

24. Study skills. The ways in which children study influence how much they learn. Teachers can often help children develop better study skills.

25. Quantity of homework. Student achievement rises significantly when teachers regularly assign homework and students conscientiously do it.

26. Quality of homework. Well-designed homework assignments relate directly to classwork and extend students' learning beyond the classroom. Homework is most useful when teachers carefully prepare the assignment, thoroughly explain it, and give prompt comments and criticism when the work is completed.

27. Assessment. Frequent and systematic monitoring of students' progress helps students, parents, teachers, administrators, and policy makers to identify strengths and weaknesses in learning and instruction.

Schools:

28. Effective schools. The most important characteristics of effective schools are strong instructional leadership, a safe and orderly climate, schoolwide emphasis on basic skills, high teacher expectations for student achievement, and continuous assessment of student progress.

29. School climate. Schools that encourage academic achievement focus on the importance of scholastic success and on maintaining order and discipline.

30. Discipline. Schools contribute to their students' academic achievement by establishing, communicating, and enforcing fair and consistent discipline policies.

31. Unexcused absences. Unexcused absences decrease when parents are promptly informed that their children are not attending school.

32. Effective principals. Successful principals establish policies that create an orderly environment and support effective instruction.

33. Collegiality. Students benefit academically when their teachers share ideas, cooperate in activities, and assist one another's intellectual growth.
34. Teacher supervision. Teachers welcome professional suggestions about improving their work, but they rarely receive them.
35. Cultural literacy. Students read more fluently and with greater understanding if they have background knowledge of the past and present. Such knowledge and understanding is called cultural literacy.
36. History. Skimpy requirements and declining enrollments in history classes are contributing to a decline in students' knowledge of the past.
37. Foreign languages. The best way to learn a foreign language in school is to start early and to study it intensively over many years.
38. Rigorous courses. The stronger the emphasis on academic courses, the more advanced the subject matter, and the more rigorous the textbooks, the more high school students learn. Subjects that are learned mainly in school rather than at home, such as science and math, are most influenced by the number and kind of courses taken.
39. Acceleration. Advancing gifted students at a faster pace results in their achieving more than similarly gifted students who are taught at a normal rate.
40. Extracurricular activities. High school students who complement their academic studies with extracurricular activities gain experience that contributes to their success in college.
41. Preparation for work. Business leaders report that students with solid basic skills and positive work attitudes are more likely to find and keep jobs than students with vocational skills alone.

(Excerpted from *What Works*, pp. 7-62)

A revised edition of *What Works* published a year later (1987) contains an additional 18 findings, which are listed below under the same three categories.

Home:
1. Television. Excessive television viewing is associated with low academic achievement. Moderate viewing, especially when supervised by parents, can help children learn.

Classroom:
2. Cooperative Learning. Students in cooperative learning teams learn to work toward a common goal, help one another learn, gain self-

esteem, take more responsibility for their own learning, and come to respect and like their classmates.

3. Solving word problems. Students will become more adept at solving math problems if teachers encourage them to think through a problem before they begin working on it, guide them through the thinking process, and give them regular and frequent practice in solving problems.

4. Vocabulary instruction. Children learn vocabulary better when the words they study are related to familiar experiences and to knowledge they already possess.

5. Illustrations. Well-chosen diagrams, graphs, photos, and illustrations can enhance students' learning.

6. Reading aloud. Hearing good readers read aloud and encouraging students repeatedly to read a passage aloud helps them become good readers.

7. Attaining competence. As students acquire knowledge and skill, their thinking and reasoning take on distinct characteristics. Teachers who are alert to these changes can determine how well their students are progressing toward becoming competent thinkers and problem solvers.

8. Behavior problems. Good classroom management is essential for teachers to deal with students who chronically misbehave, but such students also benefit from specific suggestions from teachers on how to cope with their conflicts and frustrations. This also helps them gain insights about their own behavior.

9. Purposeful writing. Students become more interested in writing and the quality of their writing improves when there are significant learning goals for writing assignments and a clear sense of purpose for writing.

10. Teacher feedback. Constructive feedback from teachers, including deserved praise and specific suggestions, helps students learn, as well as develop positive self-esteem.

11. Prior knowledge. When teachers introduce new subject matter, they need to help students grasp its relationship to facts and concepts they have previously learned.

School:

12. Character education. Good character is encouraged by surrounding students with good adult examples and by building upon natural occasions for learning and practicing good character. Skillful educators know how to organize their schools, classrooms, and lessons to foster such examples.

13. Libraries. The use of libraries enhances reading skills and encourages independent learning.
14. Attendance. A school staff that provides encouragement and personalized attention and monitors daily attendance can reduce unexcused absences and class-cutting.
15. Succeeding in a new school. When schools provide comprehensive orientation programs for students transferring from one school to another, they ease the special stresses and adjustment difficulties those students face. The result is apt to be improved student performance.
16. Instructional support. Underachieving or mildly handicapped students can benefit most from remedial education when the lessons in those classes are closely coordinated with those in their regular classes.
17. Mainstreaming. Many children who are physically handicapped or have emotional or learning problems can be given an appropriate education in well-supported regular classes and schools.
18. School to work transition. Handicapped high school students who seek them are more likely to find jobs after graduation when schools prepare them for careers and private sector businesses provide on-the-job training.

(Excerpted from *What Works*, 2nd edition, pp. 13-76)

Many educators would say the findings reported in *What Works* are mostly common sense and, for the most part, are less controversial than some of those presented in the other reviews in this chapter. For example, the finding that children improve their reading ability by reading a lot is not likely to be disputed; but Walberg's finding that class size is not directly associated with pupil learning would not be accepted by many educators.

Some would say *What Works* is partly moralistic and perhaps reflects political ideology: "Belief in the value of hard work, the importance of personal responsibility, and the importance of education itself contributes to success in school." Nevertheless, this compilation of research from the Department of Education does provide a myriad of seemingly reasonable and, according to the compiler, validated educational practices.

Limitations of Research on Effective Educational Practices

As with much educational research, and specifically with that reported in this chapter, there are shortcomings. One is using limited dependent measures to determine effectiveness — usually standardized test scores in basic skills. Another is overgeneralizing from small samples. A third is trying to determine the effects of practice by using average measures for a whole school or a whole class rather than disaggregating data for subgroups or even individuals. A fourth is overdependency on correlational studies. Most of these limitations are endemic to educational research.

Another limitation deserves special mention, since it is directly relevant to some of the research reported in this chapter. This is the practice of selectively reporting research that promotes one's personal or political bias and excluding that which fails to support or even contradicts it. For example, Glass (1987) is critical of the U.S. Department of Education's *What Works* for failing to report many significant research findings because, according to Glass, they either did not mirror the conservative educational policy of the Reagan administration or they would require substantial financial support for their implementation. Glass charges that *What Works* gives too much credibility to research and opinion that supported the federal education agenda at the time (hard work, self-discipline, teaching of phonics, and solid basic skills) while omitting research and opinion not in federal favor (open education, cooperative learning, social promotion, and small class size).

One unfortunate outcome of selective reporting of research is that practitioners wanting to improve practice might undertake to implement research findings without having the complete picture.

How Research on Effective Educational Practices Can Inform Teachers and Teacher Educators

By knowing the research on what constitutes the most effective educational practices, teachers can evaluate their own practices and perhaps modify them. As intelligent consumers of research, teachers can help to guide the development of policy and practice in their own schools and school systems. There exists no "consumer's union" for teachers, which subjects educational practices to rigorous scientific scrutiny. By knowing the research, teachers have a basis for assessing the claims of producers of instructional materials as well as those of the advocates of a particular instructional method.

For teacher educators, knowledge of the research on effective educational practices is essential in their preparation of teachers. The teacher preparation curriculum must acknowledge and espouse the best practices.

General methods courses should focus on research-based practices as reported by Walberg, Ellson, Slavin, and the U.S. Department of Education. These include reinforcement, acceleration, cues and feedback, cooperative learning, personalized instruction, adaptive instruction, tutoring, graded homework, class morale, and home intervention; also nonconventional teaching practices such as programmed learning, programmed teaching, and performance-based instruction deserve attention.

Similarly, special methods courses in various subject areas should focus on research-based practices: Reading Training, Science Mastery Learning, College-Bound Project Method (Math-English), Algorithmization Technique (Russian), and so on. The *Encyclopedia of Educational Research* (Mitzel 1982) and the *Handbook of Research on Teaching* (Wittrock 1986) are additional sources for information on effective practices for teaching content areas.

Furthermore, since both teachers and prospective teachers are influenced by what is published in professional journals, the authors who write for these journals and the editors who select what is published have an obligation to incorporate research-based practices wherever it is appropriate.

References

Brickell, H. *Commissioner's Catalog of Educational Change*. Albany: New York State Education Department, 1961.

Callahan, J.F., and Clark, L.H. *Innovations and Issues in Education*. New York: Macmillan, 1977.

Department of Classroom Teachers, American Educational Research Association of the National Education Association. *What Research Says to the Teacher Series*. Washington, D.C.: National Education Association, 1954-1967.

Ellson, D. "Improving Productivity in Teaching." *Phi Delta Kappan* 68 (October 1986): 111-24.

Glass, G. "What Works: Politics and Research." *Educational Researcher* 16 (April 1987): 5-10.

Goodlad, J.I. *School Curriculum Reform in the United States*. New York: Fund for the Advancement of Education, 1964.

Mitzel, H.E., ed. *Encyclopedia of Educational Research*. New York: Free Press, 1982.

National Education Association. *Schools for the 60s*. New York: McGraw-Hill, 1963.

Slavin, R. "Making Chapter 1 Make a Difference." *Phi Delta Kappan* 69 (October 1987): 110-19.

Slavin, R., and Madden, N. "What Works for Students At Risk: A Research Synthesis." *Educational Leadership* 46 (February 1989): 4-13.

Stevenson, H. *Comparisons of Japanese, Taiwanese and American Mathematics Achievement*. Stanford, Calif.: Center for Advanced Study in the Behavioral Sciences, 1983.

Trump, J.L., and Baynham, D. *Guide to Better Schools: Focus on Change*. Chicago: Rand McNally, 1961.

Unruh, G.G., and Alexander, W.M. *Innovations in Secondary Education*. New York: Holt, Rinehart and Winston, 1970.

U.S. Department of Education. *What Works: Research About Teaching and Learning*. Washington, D.C., 1986, revised 1987.

Walberg, H.J. "What Works in a Nation Still at Risk." *Educational Leadership* 44 (September 1986): 7-10.

Walberg, H. "Improving the Productivity of America's Schools." *Educational Leadership* 41 (May 1984): 19-27.

Wittrock, M.C., ed. *Handbook of Research on Teaching*, 3rd ed. New York: Macmillan, 1986.

4 The Search for Knowledge About Effective Teaching

An effective teacher is one judged by significant others as meeting their expectations or needs. Significant others include pupils, parents, colleagues, administrators, and the public at large. However, perceptions of what constitutes teacher effectiveness may differ from one group to another.

For pupils, effective teachers are those who help them succeed academically or socially and who make school a satisfying workplace. Parents undoubtedly feel much the same. Colleagues or peers tend to extol teachers who teach the way they do or who hold a similar teaching philosophy. Supervisors or administrators generally laud teachers who are liked by pupils, parents, and peers, who get results as measured by learning gains, and who maintain orderly classrooms with minimal disruptions. Finally, the public at large mostly is concerned with pupil learning gains and minimal disruptions both in school and outside.

The public is particularly laudatory of teachers who, without benefit of special resources, overcome seemingly extraordinary obstacles to help their pupils succeed, thus demonstrating that other teachers could make a difference, too, if they tried harder or were more creative. Two prototypes are Marva Collins and James Escalante. Collins' accomplishments with black children from Chicago's slums were heralded in a television special titled "Marva." Escalante, an East Los Angeles mathematics teacher whose mostly Hispanic students surpassed all expectations on a national calculus examination, was the subject of the film *Stand and Deliver* and the book *Escalante: The Best Teacher in America* (Mathews 1988).

These varying expectations make the definition of an effective teacher difficult. Also, definitions of teacher effectiveness often are bound by time and place. In other words, as priorities in education change, different kinds of teachers move into and out of the effective teacher "spotlight." Since

Sputnik and the *Coleman Report* (see Chapter Two), the spotlight has been on teachers who are good at producing gains in academic achievement, particularly in the basics.

The never-ending search for effective teachers stems from the strongly held belief that these teachers have a significant impact on at least the short-term outcomes of schooling, namely pupil learning and satisfaction. As a consequence, school systems want to recruit as many of these kinds of teachers as they can find and then retain them. At the same time, teacher education institutions are challenged to prepare more of them. To do so, they must have information regarding how effective teachers teach and what they are like as persons. The latter is critical for selecting candidates for preservice teacher education; the former is essential for establishing the content of the teacher preparation curriculum.

Research Approaches for Identifying Effective Teachers

Attempts to identify effective teachers have followed two approaches reflecting distinctly different eras in the history of research on teaching (Cruickshank 1986). The first approach, used prior to about 1960, focused primarily on identifying teacher traits or characteristics considered exemplary in the view of administrators and supervisors. Medley (1982) suggests the work of Kratz (1896), Charters and Waples (1929), Hart (1936), Boyce (1915), Barr (1935), and Barr and Emans (1930) as being representative. The questions investigated during this period included: To what extent do teacher evaluators agree on the characteristics of good teachers? To what extent do administrators agree when evaluating the same teacher? Can good teachers be separated from poor ones on the basis of such characteristics and ratings?

Barr and his colleagues (1961) examined and synthesized the numerous lists of exemplary characteristics of teachers contained in teacher rating instruments of the time and grouped them into 15 categories: buoyancy, consideration, cooperativeness, dependability, emotional stability, ethical behavior, expressiveness, flexibility, forcefulness, judgment, mental alertness, objectivity, personal magnetism, physical drive, and scholarship.

The problems with rating scales of exemplary characteristics are legion (Howsam 1960). Items on the scales were derived subjectively, often based on personal bias. The items were not necessarily agreed on by persons other than those devising the rating scale, thus contributing to low reliability. Also, the meaning of items on a scale was frequently vague. Take, for example, one of Barr's 15 categories such as "buoyancy." Because the term is vague, raters must guess its meaning. Different raters with somewhat different perceptions of the meaning of this term will produce different teacher ratings. To avoid this problem calls for more precise, lower-inference concepts; or the higher inference term must be operationally defined. Additionally, the scale items typically were not related to pupil learning outcome measures and thus had low validity.

Research using such rating scales to determine who are good teachers and to differentiate between good and poor ones produced mostly disappointing results. Notably, multiple raters often failed to rate the same teacher similarly; and teachers judged *a priori* to be good could not be distinguished from poor teachers on the basis of such ratings. By the end of the first era of research on teacher effectiveness based on rating scales of teacher traits or characteristics, the literature is sprinkled with conclusions such as the following:

- "There is no general agreement as to what constitutes the essential characteristics of a competent teacher" (Marsh and Wilder 1954, p. 3).
- "People cannot expect to be in close agreement when they evaluate teaching" (Howsam 1960, p. 11).
- "Traits or characteristics, taken by themselves, cannot be used to predict teacher effectiveness, nor have researchers been successful in combining the traits in such a way that they produce a useful index" (Howsam 1960, p. 26).
- "Few, if any, facts are now deemed established about teacher effectiveness and many former findings have been repudiated. It is not an exaggeration to say that we do not know today how to select, train for, or evaluate teacher effectiveness" (Biddle and Ellena 1964, p. vi).

With the onset of the Sixties, research on teacher effectiveness took a different approach (Cruickshank 1986). Rather than looking for teacher characteristics or traits *assumed* to be important for teaching, researchers turned their attention to identifying specific teacher behaviors present or operative when pupils were succeeding. Several things abetted this new approach to studying teacher effectiveness. First, there was strong motivation to counter the *Coleman Report* findings and prove that teachers, indeed, do make a difference. Second, as noted in Chapter One, several models for guiding research appeared that could be used to study direct and indirect relationships between and among the principal variables operating in the teaching-learning environment (Dunkin and Biddle 1974; McDonald and Elias 1976; Medley 1982). Third has been the advent of many classroom observation instruments to study teacher and learner behaviors.

The advent of instruments to record specific classroom behaviors and thus permit systematic analysis of what a teacher and/or pupil does has been a significant development in studying teacher effectiveness. With these observation instruments, it is possible to determine *how and to what extent teachers perform a group of precise actions and the extent to which per-forming these actions is related to other desirable attendant classroom events and/or to pupil learning.* For example, these instruments permit observers to record reliably such things as the incidence of "teacher talk" and to note its relationship to pupil learning. It was found that teacher talk constitutes one-half to two-thirds of all classroom interaction time, that student teachers talk less after teaching for a time, and that the amount of teacher talk is not closely related to pupil learning (see Dunkin and Biddle 1974).

What Have We Learned from Research on Teacher Effectiveness?

Following are 10 reviews of research on teacher effectiveness compiled in the Seventies and Eighties. As in Chapter Two, they are presented in chronological order.

Rosenshine and Furst (1971)

Purpose: To identify teacher behaviors consistently associated with pupil learning.

Method: Aggregated and reviewed 50 studies designed to find out what teacher classroom behaviors (variables) are associated with pupil learning.

Findings: Three sets of findings are reported: 1) variables found to be most promising, 2) variables found to be somewhat promising, and 3) variables for which there is little or no support.

I. Most promising teacher behavior variables
1. Clarity. Seven studies investigated this variable and all found it to have a strong, positive relationship to pupil learning.
2. Organization. Six studies found a strong, positive relationship to pupil learning.
3. Enthusiasm. Five studies found a strong, positive relationship to pupil learning.
4. Task-oriented, achievement-oriented, and/or businesslike behavior. Of seven studies, six found strong, positive relationship to pupil learning.
5. Student opportunity to learn the criterion material. Of four studies, three found a strong, positive association to pupil learning.
6. Variability. The number of studies analyzed and the number finding strong, positive relationships are not reported.

II. Somewhat promising teacher behavior variables
1. Use of pupil ideas. Of eight studies, seven found positive relation-ships with pupil learning. None found strong, positive relationships.

2. General indirectness, a category Rosenshine uses for investigations of classroom emotional climate. Five studies found positive relationships with pupil learning. A sixth study noted a strong, positive relationship.
3. Ratio of indirect to direct behaviors (see Amidon and Flanders 1963) is the incidence of one set of teacher behaviors termed "indirect" (acceptance of pupil feelings, praise and encouragement, acceptance of pupil ideas and questions) compared to a second set of behaviors termed "direct" (lecturing, giving directions, criticizing, and justifying authority). Of 13 studies, 11 found positive relationships with pupil learning. Another study found a strong, positive relationship.
4. Supportiveness. Four studies. It is unclear how many found positive relationships.
5. Criticism. Of 17 studies, 12 found a negative association and five a strong, negative relationship to pupil learning. Thus absence of criticism is a somewhat promising variable.
6. Use of structuring comments. Rosenshine does not provide data for this category.
7. Types of questions asked. Rosenshine and Furst did not report the total number of studies but noted that three indicated a strong, positive association between use of higher-order questions and pupil learning.
8. Probing questions. The description provided is not sufficient to determine the number of studies or the number having associations or strong associations with pupil learning.
9. Difficulty of instruction as related to ability of learners. Of four studies, two showed a positive association and two showed a strong, positive association with pupil learning.

III. Teacher behavior variables for which there is little or no support

Rosenshine and Furst provide a list of other teacher and pupil variables for which they could find no support. Two things are worthy of note. First, the *amount* of a quality seems to be less important than its appropriate use. For example, the amount of praise is less important than how and when it is used. Second, some of the variables have not been investigated sufficiently. However, Rosenshine and Furst believe that these preliminary findings should be reported to guide practitioners and researchers. Following is the list of variables for which there is little or no support.

1. nonverbal approval (amount)
2. praise (amount)
3. warmth (rating)
4. flexibility (amount)
5. teacher talk (amount)

6. pupil talk (amount)
7. student participation (rating)
8. teacher-pupil interactions (amount)
9. pupil absence (amount)
10. teacher absence (amount)
11. teacher preparation time (amount)
12. teacher experiences (amount)
13. teacher knowledge of subject (amount)

Comment: Heath and Nielson (1974) fault the review of Rosenshine and Furst for several logical, critical, and statistical inconsistencies and then conclude in accordance with Coleman and others that "given the well documented, strong association between student achievement and variables such as socio-economic status and ethnic status, the effects of techniques of teaching on achievement are likely to be inherently trivial" (p. 481). However, other reviewers mostly support the methodology and findings of this aggregation of studies.

Dunkin and Biddle (1974)

Purpose: To produce a non-technical textbook on teaching based on the findings of research rather than on common sense and personal beliefs.

Method: Aggregated and reviewed more than 2,000 studies that dealt mostly with some common aspect of teacher behavior (use of criticism) or some classroom phenomenon (discipline)

Findings:

1. Teacher use of criticism is to be avoided.

2. To maintain pupil involvement and to avoid pupil deviancy during recitations, teachers should demonstrate momentum, with-itness, group alerting, smoothness, accountability, overlapping, and valence and challenge arousal. Brief definitions of these teacher behaviors follow, but the reader is referred to the original investigator for fuller descriptions of these phenomena (Kounin 1970).

Momentum refers to the teacher's pacing of a lesson in order to cover the lesson objectives without digressions or distraction by pupils.

With-itness refers to the teacher's skill in being alert to all that is going on in the classroom regardless of how many activities are taking place.

Group alerting refers to the teacher's efforts to secure pupils' attention and keep them on their toes, including those who don't volunteer.

Smoothness refers to a teacher's ability to move from one activity to another without being distracted by irrelevant matters.

Accountability is the degree to which teachers hold pupils accountable and responsible for their performance.

Overlapping is the ability to handle more than one matter at the same time, such as dealing with an interruption while maintaining the lesson flow.

Valence and challenge refer to a teacher's efforts to generate pupils' enthusiasm and get them involved in their lesson.

3. To maintain pupil involvement during seatwork, teachers should use variety in teaching methods, grouping arrangements, and use of materials and should demonstrate smoothness, valence and challenge arousal, and with-itness. To avoid pupil distraction during seatwork, teachers also should demonstrate momentum, group alerting, and overlapping.

4. Acceptable classroom behavior is reinforced by appropriate use of praise, material incentives, response manipulation, and peer manipulation. Response manipulation refers to teachers not allowing pupils to do things they prefer until after they have completed assigned tasks. Peer manipulation refers to using peer pressure to get all members of a group to perform in order to receive rewards or praise.

5. Use of small groups should be encouraged only when group activities are supervised to keep pupils on target.

6. Use of more active roles for pupils is recommended.

7. Increase teacher clarity and reduce vagueness.

Cruickshank (1976)

Purpose: To compare and contrast results of relatively large-scale, federally funded research on teaching reported at the Research on Teacher Effects Conference held at the University of Texas in November 1975.

Method: Research reported in conference papers presented by Berliner and Tikunoff, Brophy and Evertson, Gage, McDonald, Stallings, and Ward and Tikunoff were compared in terms of their purposes, methodologies, variables studied, and results. (Condensations of the papers appear as articles in the Spring 1976 issue of the *Journal of Teacher Education*).

Findings:

I. Correlates of reading improvement

As reported by Berliner and Tikunoff:

1. Second- and fifth-grade reading improvement is associated with teachers who are more satisfied, accepting, attentive, encouraging, optimistic, democratic, aware of pupil developmental levels, consistent in controlling the class, tolerant of race and class, equitable in dividing time among pupils, and knowledgeable about teaching reading. Additionally, they provide more structure for the learner, capitalize on unexpected events, show more warmth, wait for pupils to answer questions, make pupils responsible for their work, use more praise, adjust to the learner's rate, monitor, use less

busy work, make fewer illogical statements, are less belittling, less har-rassing, less ignoring, less recognition seeking. Their pupils move around more, are more cooperative, more engaged, manipulate the teacher less, and are less defiant. Classrooms are more convivial and involve other adults to help during instruction.

2. Effective second-grade compared with effective fifth-grade teachers use more positive reinforcement, move around more, are more open, ask more open-ended and interpretive questions, are more trustful, call more pupils by name, are more polite, and use more teacher-made materials. They promote less competition, do less stereotyping, less moralizing, less polic-ing, less rushing, less shaming, are less concerned about time, and are less sarcastic.

3. Effective fifth-grade teachers compared with effective second-grade teachers tend to defend their pupils, utilize pupil peer teaching, do less drilling, and exclude or banish pupils less.

As reported by McDonald:

1. Second-grade reading instruction is enhanced by use of small-group instruction, use of a variety of instructional materials, constant teacher monitoring and corrective feedback, ability of the teacher to maximize di-rect instructional time and to maintain a high level of interaction with pupils not in the reading group.

2. Fifth-grade reading instruction is best accomplished where teachers spend considerable time explaining, questioning, and stimulating cognitive processes, where there is considerable independent work, and where the teacher uses instructional variety.

As reported by Stallings:

1. First- and third-grade improvement in reading is associated with: the length of the school day and time spent on reading, greater interactions be-tween adults and pupils, positive pupil reinforcement, task persistence as exhibited by pupils working by themselves, and use of textbooks and pro-grammed workbooks.

II. Correlates of language arts and mathematics improvement

As reported by Brophy:

1. Second- and third-grade teachers whose pupils do well in both lan-guage arts and math seem to take into account pupil socioeconomic status (SES). In high SES schools effective teachers are task-oriented and keep pupils on task, have high expectations, are demanding and critical. They "push" pupils and teach in traditional ways. In low SES schools effective teachers have high expectations for pupils; are more supportive, encourag-

ing, and affectively oriented; are willing to reteach; take up pupils' personal matters; and look for materials that work.

III. Correlates of math improvement
As reported by Berliner and Tikunoff:

1. Second- and fifth-grade math improvement is associated with teachers who are more accepting, attentive to learners, consistent in controlling the classroom, knowledgeable about math, optimistic, and polite. They monitor learning, ask more open-ended questions, adjust to the learner's rate, capitalize on unexpected events, call pupils by name, make pupils responsible for their work, and provide more structure. They are less abrupt and belittling, do not seek recognition, do not banish or exclude pupils, use less "busy work," make fewer illogical statements, do not treat the class as a whole, and use less sarcasm and shaming. Their pupils are more cooperative, engaged, and less defiant. Classrooms are more cooperative and convivial, and other adults are used to help with instruction.

2. Effective second-grade compared with effective fifth-grade math teachers are more democratic, encouraging, warm, flexible, and satisfied. They are more aware of pupils' developmental levels. They are more equitable in dividing time among pupils, move around more, use more praise, individualize, use pupil peer teaching, and wait for pupils to answer questions. They show more warmth, are not influenced by the way pupils have been characterized in the past, do not place undue emphasis on quietness, care less about being liked, are less distrustful, harassing, ignoring, moralizing, and are less concerned about time.

3. Effective fifth-grade teachers compared with effective second-grade teachers use more positive reinforcement and less nonverbal control behavior. Their pupils are less manipulative.

As reported by McDonald:

1. Effective second-grade math instruction is characterized by more time spent on math, more monitoring of individual pupil work, keeping pupils on-task, and teaching a wide variety of content and skills.

2. Effective fifth-grade math instruction includes use of both small-group and whole-class teaching and use of a variety of instructional techniques.

As reported by Stallings:

1. First- and third-grade math instruction seems to be enhanced by a longer school day and more time spent on math learning, by frequent use of textbooks, programmed workbooks, Cuisenaire rods, and Montessori materials; also when teacher and pupils often discuss mathematics, when instruction is systematic, and when teachers provide immediate reinforcement.

2. Small-group instruction is more effective in first grade and large-group instruction is more effective in third grade.

As reported by Ward and Tikunoff
1. Fourth- and fifth-grade pupils who are below grade level in mathematics are not significantly aided by tutoring. (This finding is in contrast to support for tutoring reported in Chapter Two.)

Medley (1977)

Purpose: To provide teacher educators access to the research-based findings about effective teaching.

Method: Reviewed 289 studies that purportedly dealt with how the behavior of effective teachers differs from that of ineffective teachers. Applied four criteria in selecting usable studies: 1) the findings had to be generalizable to some population of teachers larger than the sample from which the data was obtained; 2) the findings had to be statistically significant (+ or − .387) and practically significant in terms of substantial improvement in pupil achievement and perhaps with cost-benefits as well; 3) the findings had to be based on long-term pupil gains in achievement areas recognized as important to education; and 4) the process measures or independent variables studied had to be low enough inference that they could be reproduced, that is, they had to be defined operationally. Only 14 of the 289 studies met all four criteria.

General findings:
1. A competent teacher of subject matter is likely to develop positive pupil attitudes toward school.
2. Teachers who achieve maximum pupil gains are also likely to improve pupils' self-concepts.
3. Behaviors of effective teachers of reading and mathematics in the first three grades are very similar.
4. Behavior patterns of teachers effective with low SES pupils differ considerably from those of teachers effective with high SES pupils (one study only).

Specific findings for effective teachers of low SES pupils. These teachers:
1. Devote more time to task-related, academic activities and less time to deviancy control.
2. Spend more time with large groups than with small groups.
3. Assign more seatwork.
4. Individualize assignments more.
5. Ask more questions of a lower order, factual nature.

6. Are less likely to simplify, discuss, or use pupil answers.
7. Have fewer pupil-initiated questions and comments.
8. Keep interaction at a low level of complexity and pupil initiative.
9. Have less deviant or disruptive pupil behavior.
10. Use less criticism and have a more varied repertoire of control techniques.
11. Give pupils less freedom to govern their activities.
12. Maintain an environment that, if not always quiet, is at least free from disruptive pupil behavior.
13. Spend more time and effort supervising individual pupil work.
14. If primary teachers, are more likely to ask a question and then to choose a non-volunteer to answer (a form of "group alerting").
15. If primary teachers, pay more and closer attention to individual pupils.

Specific behaviors of effective teachers of upper elementary grades. These teachers:
1. Talk more.
2. Keep pupils on task.
3. Are less permissive.
4. Permit pupils to initiate more interchanges.
5. Ask easier questions.
6. Manage with less effort.
7. Are more selective with criticism.
8. Attend to pupils less closely.
9. Favor less traditional materials.
10. Are more traditional, less exciting.

Gage (1978)

Purpose: To identify correlates of teaching effectiveness that could be included in a Stanford University experimental teacher education program.

Method: Four major studies were reviewed: Brophy and Evertson (1974), McDonald and Elias (1976), Soar and Soar (1972), and Stallings and Kaskowicz (1974).

Findings: Gage makes the following inferences as to how third-grade teachers can maximize achievement in reading and mathematics for children with either high or low academic orientations.

1. They should have a system of rules that allows pupils to attend to their personal and procedural needs without having to check with the teacher.

76

2. They should move around the room frequently to monitor pupil work and communicate to them regarding their behavior.
3. They should minimize the need for giving directions and classroom organization by placing such information, including the daily work schedule, on the chalkboard.
4. They should ensure that all pupils participate equally in answering questions.
5. They should ensure that independent work is interesting, worthwhile, and capable of being completed without too much teacher direction.
6. When teaching reading, teachers should give frequent, brief feedback and provide fast-paced activities.
7. Teachers should maximize academic learning time by actively engaging pupils in productive work.

Borich (1979)

Purpose: To report the most parsimonious and practical implications for teacher education based on five process-product studies investigating relationships between teacher behaviors and elementary school pupil achievement on standardized tests of reading and math.

Method: Five studies were reviewed: Brophy and Evertson (1974), Good and Grouws (1975), McDonald et al. (1975), Soar and Soar (1972), and Stallings and Kaskowicz (1974). The findings are summarized and then compared. Consistent and disparate findings are noted.

Findings:

From Brophy and Evertson (1974)
1. Keep pupils actively involved.
2. Establish flexible rules for order.
3. Use mild, non-physical punishment.
4. Take responsibility for pupil achievement or lack of it, have high expectations.
5. Vary the difficulty of the lesson as necessary.
6. Call on pupils systematically rather than randomly.
7. Give credit for partially correct answers.
8. Give feedback.
9. Encourage question asking.

For low SES pupils:
1. Be warm and encouraging.
2. Provide adequate pupil response time.
3. Present information in small chunks at a slow pace.

4. Stress factual knowledge.
5. Monitor pupil progress.
6. Minimize interruptions.
7. Provide smooth transitions.
8. Provide help immediately to those who need it.
9. Use special materials to meet individual needs.

For high SES pupils:
1. Correct wrong or poor answers.
2. Ask difficult questions.
3. Follow the curriculum.
4. Assign homework.
5. Let pupils initiate questions and projects.
6. Encourage the reasoning out of answers.

From Good and Grouws (1975)
1. Maximize whole-class instruction.
2. Maintain a relaxed atmosphere.
3. Establish work and success standards for pupils and maintain them.
4. Provide feedback.
5. Ask clear questions.
6. Limit use of praise when performance is poor or when pupil expectations are low.
7. Encourage pupil-initiated contacts with teacher.
8. Maintain a classroom free of major behavioral problems.

From McDonald et al. (1975)
1. Maximize direct instruction during second-grade reading by using small-group procedures and by maintaining a high level of interaction with individual pupils.
2. Maximize content coverage in second-grade math instruction.
3. Reduce group work and increase individual monitoring of pupils during math instruction in fifth grade.
4. Discuss, explain, question, stimulate during fifth-grade reading.

From Soar and Soar (1972)
1. Use moderate control techniques.
2. Vary structure. Increase it for low and decrease it for higher cognitive objectives.
3. Vary teacher-pupil interaction according to pupils' needs and abilities.
4. Increase positive affect for low SES pupils. Lower it for high SES pupils.

From Stallings and Kaskowicz (1974)
1. Maximize instructional time.
2. Use systematic instruction (present content, ask questions, wait for responses, provide feedback, guide pupils to correct responses).
3. Encourage discussion of mathematics material.
4. Encourage and praise pupils with low mathematics achievement.
5. Use textbooks and programmed workbooks for math instruction.
6. Encourage task persistence during math instruction.
7. Use a wide variety of instructional materials.
8. Encourage pupil accountability.

Good (1979)

Purpose: To summarize what is known about effectiveness among elementary teachers.
Method: Reviewed selected studies.
Findings:
1. Teachers' managerial abilities are positively related to pupil achievement in every study. However, although managerial skills are necessary, they are not sufficient to ensure pupil learning.
2. Teachers manage classrooms so as to maximize pupil task involvement and to minimize disruption.
3. Teachers who structure and monitor learning do better at teaching basic skills.
4. Direct instruction is associated with increased pupil learning gains. Direct instruction implies orderly classrooms, persistence on academic tasks, active involvement with pupils, and a structured learning situation.

Emmer and Evertson (1982)

Purpose: To identify what is known about the behavior of teachers who are effective classroom managers.
Method: Aggregated studies wherein teacher behaviors were identified that were related to high levels of pupil involvement in class activities, minimal amounts of pupil behavior that interfere with or disrupt instruction, and efficient use of instructional time.
Findings:
1. During recitations pupils are more involved and less prone to misbehavior when teachers exhibit momentum, with-itness, smoothness, and group alerting.

2. During seatwork pupils are less prone to misbehavior when teachers exhibit with-itness, momentum, and smoothness. Pupils will be more involved in their work when teachers provide variety in seatwork.
3. Pupils are more likely to be on task during activities led and paced by the teacher than during independent seatwork.
4. Teacher behaviors associated with greater pupil involvement in lessons include use of more feedback, more focused and substantive interaction with academic content, greater structuring during math instruction, and use of prompting, structured transitions, questions, incentives, and appropriate pacing.
5. When beginning the school year, elementary teachers establish behavioral expectations for pupils, monitor behavior regularly, deal with inappropriate behavior promptly, provide clear directions and presentations, listen, and express feelings.
6. When beginning the school year, junior high teachers set work expectations and standards, establish appropriate behaviors, monitor and deal with inappropriate behavior promptly, accept and use pupil ideas, and joke and smile.

Stallings (1982)

Purpose: To review studies that isolate effective strategies for helping low-achieving secondary school pupils.
Method: Reviewed selected studies.
Findings:
1. In a study of 102 junior high school mathematics/English classrooms, effective classroom managers had clear plans for the first day. Specifically, they:
   a. made procedures, rules, and consequences clear.
   b. held pupils responsible and accountable.
   c. were skillful in providing instruction and information.
   d. were skillful in organizing multiple instructional activities.
2. In a study of 14 secondary schools, more effective classroom managers were:
   a. efficient in making assignments and dispensing materials resulting in more instructional time.
   b. were prompt in starting class and continued teaching until the end of class.
   c. when working with pupils who read below fourth-grade level, were likely to spend more time in oral reading in small groups

and to devote to more time to use of examples and providing explanations (clarity), reviewing, and discussing.

   d. were more likely to use oral instruction when introducing new work, to discuss and review, to provide directed practice, to question, to acknowledge correct answers and correct wrong answers supportively, and to include all pupils.

3. Effective classroom managers use certain school procedures to help low-achieving pupils. They include:

   a. maintaining classroom climate that is friendly, competitive, and with high expectations.

   b. whole-class teaching with pupils sometimes leading, giving reports, reading aloud.

   c. keeping intrusions to a minimum.

   d. assigning pupils to smaller, homogeneously grouped classes.

   e. giving pupils grades based on progress rather than on attainment of grade-level standards.

   f. encouraging parent interest and participation in their child's program and progress.

Porter and Brophy (1988)

Purpose: To synthesize research on good teaching, especially from the work of the Institute for Research on Teaching at Michigan State University.

Method: Identification of a number of macro-level findings from research on teaching conducted since 1976 at the Institute for Research on Teaching.

Findings:

1. Effective teachers have the ability to plan and negotiate a number of classroom goals. They seem to be able to accomplish both academic and socialization goals. They integrate content and skills learning.

2. Effective teachers know their subject and their pupils; they display instructional and classroom management skills and other behaviors associated with effective pedagogy.

3. Effective teachers accept personal responsibility for pupil learning and behavior. They engage in corrective, problem-solving approaches with failing pupils rather than punishing them for their shortcomings.

4. Effective teachers make clear what is to be learned and how it relates to what has been learned previously or what will be learned in the future.

5. Effective teachers explicitly model and instruct pupils in information processing, sense-making, and problem-solving. They show

pupils how to think and give them opportunities to do so. They monitor comprehension regularly.

6. Effective teachers anticipate and correct misconceptions pupils have about their world.
7. Effective teachers carefully select and use instructional materials to fit the curriculum goals and pupil characteristics. They clarify and expand on such materials to enrich the curriculum.
8. Effective teachers are reflective. They take time to think about what, why, and how they are teaching.

Table 7 on pages 84-85 indicates which studies had similar findings.

Summary of Effective Teaching Research

The effective teacher behaviors identified in the 10 studies summarized here can be organized into seven clusters: 1) teacher character traits, 2) what the teacher knows, 3) what the teacher teaches, 4) what the teacher expects, 5) how the teacher teaches, 6) how the teacher reacts to pupils, and 7) how the teacher manages the classroom. Following is a discussion of each of these clusters, which can serve as a tentative listing of the variables constituting teacher effectiveness.

Teacher character traits. A large number of items associated with teacher effectiveness identified in the various reviews of research are teacher character traits. They suggest that teachers are effective when they are: enthusiastic, stimulating, encouraging, warm, task-oriented and businesslike, tolerant-polite-tactful, trusting, flexible-adaptable, and democratic. Also, they hold high expectations for pupils, do not seek personal recognition, care less about being liked, are able to overcome pupil stereotypes, are less time-conscious, feel responsible for pupil learning, are able to express feelings, and have good listening skills.

What the teacher knows. The reviews of research suggest that effective teachers need to know many things and be skilled in using that knowledge. Specifically, effective teachers are knowledgeable in their subject fields (disputed by Rosenshine and Furst 1971) and possess a great deal of factual information. In addition, many kinds of knowledge and skill are inferred in the clusters that follow.

What the teacher teaches. The reviews of research suggest that effective teachers ensure coverage of the criterion material for which pupils are accountable and go beyond it to provide maximal content coverage.

How the teacher teaches. This cluster includes a large number of effective behaviors related to the act of teaching. The reviews of research suggest that effective teachers demonstrate clarity, provide variety, establish

82

and maintain momentum, make effective use of small groups, encourage more pupil participation, monitor and attend to pupils, and structure teaching and learning. Also, they take advantage of unexpected events (teachable moments), monitor seatwork, use both open-ended and lower-order questions, involve pupils in peer teaching, use programmed materials and manipulatives, use large-group instruction, avoid complexity by providing information in small chunks, use less busywork, and use fewer traditional materials. Additionally, they show pupils the importance of what is to be learned, demonstrate the thinking processes necessary for learning, anticipate and correct pupil misconceptions, and are reflective about what they are doing with respect to teaching and learning.

What the teacher expects. Two items fall into this cluster: establishing expectations for pupils and holding them accountable, and encouraging parent participation in the pupil's academic life.

How the teacher reacts to pupils. The reviews of research suggest that effective teachers are accepting and supportive, deal with pupils in a consistent manner, make little but judicious use of pupil criticism, demonstrate with-itness (aware of what is going on), make judicious use of praise, use incentives, adjust to pupil developmental levels, individualize instruction, ensure equitable pupil participation, direct questions to non-volunteers, know all of their pupils' names, use appropriate wait-time when asking questions, use prompting, give immediate feedback to help learners, are aware of and sensitive to learning differences among SES or cultural groups and adjust to these differences.

How teachers manage. The seventh cluster of effective teacher attributes is gleaned from reviews of research dealing with classroom management. Effective teachers demonstrate expertise in planning, have strong organization from the first day of class, are prompt in starting classes, make smooth transitions, are skillful in overlapping or handling two or more classroom activities concurrently, use group alerting especially to involve pupils who don't volunteer, are persistent and efficient in maintaining time-on-task, and minimize disruptions. Also, effective teachers are accepting of some "noise" in the classroom, have a repertory of control techniques, use mild forms of punishment, maintain a relaxed atmosphere, and hold pupils to work and success standards.

Shortcomings of Teacher Effectiveness Research

Research on teacher effectiveness has a number of limitations. A major one is the lack of agreement on the outcome variable to determine effectiveness. What is the primary role of teachers? Is it to instruct, to counsel,

Table 7. Promising teacher effectiveness variables in the order of their denotation in the text.

Key:
+ indicates support
– indicates negative support
NS indicates "not sure"
* contingencies affect use of

Reviews

Effective teachers seem to demonstrate:	Rosenshine & Furst	Dunkin & Biddle	Cruickshank	Medley	Gage	Borich	Good	Emmer & Evertson	Stallings	Porter & Brophy
1. Clarity	+	+	+		+	+		+	+	+
2. Organization (clarity of)	+									
3. Enthusiasm (also valence-challenge arousal)	+									
4. Task-oriented, businesslike behavior	+		+			+				
5. Provision of opportunity for students to learn criterion material	+			+		+				
6. Variability/variety	+		+			+				
7. Criticism (negatively related)*	+	+	+	+						
8. "Seatwork variety and challenge"		+			+					
9. "With-itness"		+						+		
10. "Smoothness" (of transitions)		+					+	+		
11. "Momentum" (pacing)		+						+		
12. "Overlappingness"		+							+	
13. "Group alerting"*		+			+			+		
14. "Accountability"		+	+				+			
15. Praise*	–	+	+				+			
16. Use of material incentives		+							+	
17. Use of small groups*		+					+			
18. Use of more pupil participation/ interaction*		+	+				+		+	+
19. Acceptance-support		+							+	
20. Attending/monitoring behavior		+			+	+	+			+
21. Awareness of and adjustment to developmental levels		+					+			
22. Consistency in controlling		+			+	NS			+	
23. Encouragement		+				+				
24. Tolerance-politeness-tact		+								
25. Optimism		+								
26. Equitableness of pupil participation		+			+		+		+	
27. Knowledge of subject	–	+								+
28. Structure*		+				+	+	+		
29. Ability to capture and use unexpected events (teachable moments)		+								
30. Warmth	–	NS	+			+				
31. Wait-time		+				+				
32. Individualization		+	+			+				
33. Less "busy-work"		+								
34. Time-on-task persistence and efficiency		+			+	+	+		+	
35. Use of independent work*		+								+
36. Stimulation		+				+				
37. Use of feedback		+				+		+	+	
38. High expectations		+				+				
39. Awareness of and adjustment to pupil SES		+	+			+				
40. Use of open-ended questions*	NS	+			+					
41. Call pupils by name		+								
42. Less recognition seeking		+								
43. Democratic style		+								

	Rosenshine & Furst	Dunkin & Biddle	Cruickshank	Medley	Gage	Borich	Good	Emmer & Evertson	Stallings	Porter & Brophy
44. Flexibility-adaptability	−	+								
45. Ability to overcome stereotypes of particular pupils		+								
46. Acceptance of some "noise"		+								
47. Less caring about being liked		+								
48. Trust		+								
49. Less time consciousness		+								
50. Use of pupil peer teaching		+								
51. Use of programmed materials		+								
52. Use of manipulatives		+								
53. Immediate reinforcement	+	+								
54. Large-group instruction				+		+			+	
55. More seatwork				+						
56. More lower-order questions	NS	+								
57. Less use of pupil ideas or answers			+				−			
58. Less pupil initiated talk*	NS			+		−				
59. Less complexity				+						
60. A repertory of control techniques	−			+						
61. Questioning of non-volunteers	+			+						
62. Use of less traditional materials				+						
63. Use of independent work that is interesting, worthwhile and able to be completed independently					+					
64. Use of mild forms of punishment						+				
65. Responsibility for pupil learning						+				+
66. Ability to provide information in small chunks						+				
67. Possession and use of factual knowledge						+				
68. Ability to minimize disruptions						+		+	+	
69. Provision of immediate help to learners						+				
70. Ability to maintain relaxed atmosphere						+		+	+	
71. Maintenance of pupil work and success standards						+				
72. Maximal content coverage						+				
73. Prompting								+		
74. Ability to express feelings								+		
75. Listening skills								+		
76. Organization for and from the first day									+	
77. Promptness in starting class									+	
78. Use of oral reading*									+	
79. Use of parent participation									+	
80. Planning expertise										+
81. Ability to show pupils relationship and importance of what is being learned to past and future learning										+
82. Metacognitive processes necessary for learning										+
83. Ability to anticipate and correct pupil misconceptions										+
84. Ability to select, use, enrich and expand on appropriate instructional materials										+
85. Reflectiveness										+

to manage, to bring about social change, to advance the profession of teaching? Selecting one or another of these roles will make quite a difference in the outcome variable used to define effectiveness. Suppose the role of the teacher is to make school a satisfying workplace, as suggested by Bane and Jencks (1972). Given that role, effective teaching would be demonstrated by pupil satisfaction in and with school, and it might be measured by pupil attendance and lack of tardiness. However, suppose the role of the teacher is seen primarily as one of instructing, and effectiveness is measured by pupils' academic gain on standardized tests. Given the different possible goals of teaching, we can see why there might be some disagreement about which outcome variables are measures of effectiveness.

Another shortcoming of teacher effectiveness research is the nature of the population sampled. Because of federal priorities, the target population of most government-subsidized studies has been mainly low SES pupils at the elementary level; and the teacher populations studied have been mostly volunteers. Also, in some studies the sample of both pupils and teachers has been quite small.

Still another set of shortcomings have to do with methodological problems. Among those mentioned in the literature are: 1) disagreement regarding the unit of analysis (pupil or teacher); 2) use of narrow outcome measures (typically standardized tests of basic skills) that limit generalizability and may not reflect what is taught in the curriculum; 3) use of weak research designs; 4) use of high-inference independent variables; 5) limiting the study of teacher behaviors to just frequency of occurrence rather than their appropriateness (quality and timing); 6) failure to take into account the questionable stability of teacher behaviors over time; and 7) over-dependency on correlational studies. (Correlational studies on teacher behavior typically fall in the .2 to .5 range, which although positive is not particulary strong.) These shortcomings and others are discussed more fully in Berliner (1976), Dunkin and Biddle (1974), Heath and Nielson (1974), Gage (1985), Kennedy and Bush (1976), McBee and Fortune (1978), Medley (1982), Roseshine and Furst (1971), and Scriven (1987).

How Research on Teacher Effectiveness Informs Teachers and Teacher Educators

Despite the shortcomings of teacher effectiveness research, it does seem to be finding its way into the literature and thus influencing practice. For example, the Association for Supervision and Curriculum Development has published two research-based books on the topic: *Effective Instruction* (Levin and Long 1981) and *Using What We Know About Teaching* (Hosford 1984).

86

Also, the American Association of Colleges for Teacher Education has published *Essential Knowledge for Beginning Educators* (Smith 1983) and *Knowledge Base for the Beginning Teacher* (Reynolds 1989). Perhaps most significant is that the National Council for Accreditation of Teacher Education in its *Standards* (1987) calls for all teacher education institutions "to ensure that its professional education programs are based on essential knowledge and current research findings" (p. 37).

In discussing how recently acquired knowledge of effective teaching can be applied, Gage (1985) notes it can be used foremost to improve pedagogy — the art and science of teaching — since it, in part, answers the basic question asked by both practicing and preservice teachers: How should I teach?

The task now is not merely to get the word out about how research informs teaching. Rather, it is to provide specific training opportunities whereby preservice and practicing teachers gain *both* knowledge of and skill in the behaviors research has shown to be effective. We can no longer regard the preparation of teachers as simply "education sans training" (Cruickshank and Metcalf 1990). With a knowledge base for teaching and with the widespread dissemination of that knowledge, perhaps we can convince others in positions of power that teaching is a most complex and intellectually demanding profession, which deserves greater public respect and more resources to do the job of educating America's children and youth.

References

Amidon, E.G., and Flanders, N.A. *The Role of the Teacher in the Classroom.* Minneapolis: Amidon and Associates, 1963.

Bane, M., and Jencks, C. "The Schools and Equal Opportunity." *Saturday Review of Education* 1, no. 3 (1972): 37-42.

Barr, A.S. "The Validity of Certain Instruments Employed in the Measurement of Teaching Ability." In *The Measurement of Teaching Efficiency*, edited by H.M. Walker. New York: Macmillan, 1935.

Barr, A.S., and Emans, L.M. "What Qualities Are Prerequisite to Success in Teaching?" *Nation's Schools* 6 (1930): 60-64.

Barr, A.; Worcester, D.; Abell, A.; Beecher, C.; Jensen, L.; Peronto, A.; Ringness, T.; and Schmidt, J. "Wisconsin Studies of the Measurement and Prediction of Teacher Effectiveness." *Journal of Experimental Education* 30 (September 1961): 1-156.

Berliner, D. "Impediments to the Study of Teacher Effectiveness." *Journal of Teacher Education* 27 (Spring 1976): 5-13.

Berliner, D.C., and Tikunoff, W.J. "The California Beginning Teacher Evaluation Study: Overview of the Ethnographic Study." *Journal of Teacher Education* 27 (Spring 1976): 24-30.

Biddle, B., and Ellena, W. *Contemporary Research on Teacher Effectiveness*. New York: Holt, Rinehart & Winston, 1964.

Borich, G. "Implications for Developing Teacher Competencies from Process-Product Research." *Journal of Teacher Education* 30 (Spring 1979): 77-86.

Boyce, A.C. "Methods for Measuring Teachers' Efficiency." In *Methods for Measuring Teachers' Deficiency, Fourteenth Yearbook of the National Society for the Study of Education, Part II*, edited by S.C. Parker. Bloomington, Ill.: Public School Publishing Company, 1915.

Brophy, J., and Evertson, E. *Learning from Teaching: A Developmental Perspective*. Boston: Allyn and Bacon, 1976.

Brophy, J., and Evertson, C. *Process-Product Correlations in the Texas Teacher Effectiveness Study*. Final Report No. 74-4. Austin: Research and Development Center for Teacher Education, University of Texas, 1974.

Brophy, J., and Good, T. "Teacher Behavior and Student Achievement." In *Handbook of Research on Teaching*, edited by M. Wittrock. New York: Macmillan, 1986.

Charters, W.W., and Waples, D. *The Commonwealth Teacher Training Study*. Chicago: University of Chicago Press, 1929.

Cruickshank, D. "Profile of an Effective Teacher." *Educational Horizons* 64 (Winter 1986): 80-86.

Cruickshank, D. "Syntheses of Selected Recent Research on Teacher Effects." *Journal of Teacher Education* 27 (Spring 1976): 57-61

Cruickshank, D., and Metcalf, K. "Training Within Teacher Preparation." In *Handbook of Research on Teacher Education*, edited by R. Houston et al. New York: Macmillan, 1990.

Dunkin, M.J., and Biddle, B.J. *The Study of Teaching*. New York: Holt, Rinehart & Winston, 1974. Reprinted, Washington, D.C.: University Press of America, 1982.

Emmer, E.T., and Evertson, C.M. "Synthesis of Research on Classroom Management." *Educational Leadership* 38, (January 1982): 342-47.

Gage, N.L. "A Factorially Designed Experiment on Teacher Structuring, Soliciting and Reacting." *Journal of Teacher Education* 27 (Spring 1976): 35-38.

Gage, N.L. *Hard Gains in the Soft Sciences: The Case of Pedagogy*. Bloomington, Ind.: Phi Delta Kappa, 1985.

Gage, N.L. "The Yield of Research on Teaching." *Phi Delta Kappan* 60 (November 1978): 229-35.

Good, T. "Teacher Effectiveness in the Elementary School." *Journal of Teacher Education* 30 (Summer 1979): 52-64.

Good, T., and Grouws, D. *Process-Product Relationships in 4th-Grade Mathematics Classes*. Columbia: University of Missouri College of Education, 1975.

Hart, J.W. *Teachers and Teaching*. New York: Macmillan, 1936.

Heath, R., and Nielson, M. "The Research Bases for Performance-Based Teacher Education." *Review of Educational Research* 44, no. 4 (1974): 463-84.

Hosford, P., ed. *Using What We Know About Teaching*. Alexandria, Va.: Association for Supervision and Curriculum Development, 1984.

Howsam, R. *Who's a Good Teacher?* Burlingame: California School Boards Association and the California Teachers Association, 1960.

Kennedy, J., and Bush, A. "Overcoming Some Impediments to the Study of Teacher Effectiveness." *Journal of Teacher Education* 27 (Spring 1976): 14-17.

Kounin, J.S. *Discipline and Group Management in Classrooms*. New York: Holt, 1970.

Kratz, H.E. "Characteristics of the Best Teachers as Recognized by Children." *Pedagogical Summary* (1896): 413-18.

Levin, T., and Long, R. *Effective Instruction*. Alexandria, Va.: Association for Supervision and Curriculum Development, 1981.

Mathews, J. *Escalante: The Best Teacher in America*. New York: H. Holt, 1988.

McBee, J., and Fortune, J. "Use of Distribution Parameters of Achievement Scores for Teacher Placement." *Journal of Classroom Interaction* 13, no. 2 (1978): 22-26.

McDonald, F.J. "Report on Phase II of the Beginning Teacher Evaluation Study." *Journal of Teacher Education* 27 (Spring 1976): 39-42.

McDonald, F., and Elias, P. *The Effects of Teacher Performance on Pupil Learning, Beginning Teacher Evaluation Study, Phase II*. Final Report, Volume 1. Princeton, N.J.: Educational Testing Service, 1976.

McDonald, F.; Elias, P.; Stone, M.; Wheeler, P.; Clafee, R.; Sandoval, J.; Eckstrom, R.; and Lockheed, M. *Final Report on Phase II Beginning Teacher Evaluation Study*. Princeton, N.J.: Educational Testing Service, 1975.

Medley, D. "Teacher Effectiveness." In *Encyclopedia of Educational Research*, edited by H. Mitzel. New York: Free Press, 1982.

Medley, D.M. *Teacher Competence and Teacher Effectiveness: A Review of Process-Product Research*. Washington, D.C.: American Association of Colleges for Teacher Education, 1977.

Marsh, J., and Wilder, E. *Identifying the Effective Instructor: A Review of the Quantitative Studies, 1800-1952*. Research Bulletin No. AFPATRC-TR-54-44. San Antonio, Texas: USAF Personnel Training Research Center, 1954.

National Council for Accreditation of Teacher Education. *Standards, Procedures, and Policies for the Accreditation of Professional Education Units*. Washington, D.C., 1987.

Porter, A., and Brophy, J. "Synthesis of Research on Good Teaching." *Educational Leadership* 45, no. 8 (1988): 74-85.

Reynolds, M., ed. *Knowledge Base for the Beginning Teacher*. Elmsford, N.Y.: Pergamon, 1989.

Rosenshine, B. *Teaching Behaviors and Student Achievement*. London: National Foundation for Educational Research, 1971.

Rosenshine, B., and Furst, N. "Research on Teacher Performance Criteria." In *Research in Teacher Education*, edited by B.O. Smith. Englewood Cliffs, N.J.: Prentice-Hall, 1971.

Scriven, M. "Validity in Personnel Evaluation." *Journal of Personnel Evaluation in Education* 1, no. 1 (1987): 9-23.

Smith, P., ed. *Essential Knowledge for Beginning Educators*. Washington, D.C.: American Association of Colleges for Teacher Education and ERIC Clearinghouse on Teacher Education, 1983.

Soar, R., and Soar, R. "An Empirical Analysis of Selected Follow-Through Programs." In *Early Childhood Education: Seventy-first Yearbook of the National Society for Study of Education, Part II*, edited by I. Gordon. Chicago: University of Chicago Press, 1972.

Stallings, J.A. "Effective Strategies for Teaching Basic Skills." In *Developing Basic Skills Programs in Secondary Schools*, edited by I. Gordon. Alexandria, Va.: Association for Supervision and Curriculum Development, 1982.

Stallings, J.A. "How Instructional Processes Relate to Child Outcomes in a National Study of Follow-Through." *Journal of Teacher Education* 27 (Spring 1976): 43-47.

Stallings, J., and Kaskowicz, D. *Follow-Through Classroom Observation Evaluation (1972-73)*. Menlo Park, Calif.: Stanford Research Institute, 1974.

Ward, B.A., and Tikunoff, W.J. "The Effective Teacher Education Program: Application of Selected Research Results and Methodology to Teaching." *Journal of Teacher Education* 27 (Spring 1976): 48-53.

5 The Search for Knowledge About Teacher Education

Until recently, research on teacher education has been virtually ignored in the major compilations of research literature. For example, the *Encyclopedia of Educational Research* has had no section on the topic in either its Third Edition (1960), its Fourth Edition (1969), or its Fifth Edition (1982). Similarly, one will not find any attention given to the topic in the *International Encyclopedia of Teaching and Teacher Education* (1987). Nor is attention given to the topic in the First Edition of *Handbook of Research on Teaching* (1963). Not until the Second Edition was published in 1973, do we find a chapter specifically devoted to the topic (Peck and Tucker 1973). Thirteen years later with the publication of the Third Edition we find a contribution by Lanier and Little (1986). The periodical literature also is devoid of such attention, an exception being a brief summation by Koehler (1985). Thus this author's search, with the exception of the summations by Lanier and Little and by Koehler, relies primarily on collecting and reporting the work of individual investigators. Their work is summarized in this chapter, which is organized around the five primary variables suggested by Cruickshank (1984): 1) preservice teachers, 2) preservice curriculum, 3) preservice instruction, 4) the education professoriate, and 5) the context of teacher preparation.

Preservice Teachers

Why Do Persons Elect to Teach?

In the past dozen years, a number of investigators have attempted to determine the reasons why preservice teachers choose to become teachers. Among them are Andrew (1983); Bontempo and Digman (1985); Book and

Freeman (1986); Book, Freeman, and Brousseau (1985); Horton, Daniel, and Summers (1985); Jantzen (1982); Joseph and Green (1986); Kemper and Mangieri (1985); Research About Teacher Education Project (1987); Roberson, Keith, and Page (1983); Wood (1978); and Yarger, Howey, and Joyce (1977).

To determine the reasons for choosing a career in teaching, Andrew and two colleagues analyzed papers written by 248 preservice teachers, mostly sophomores, enrolled in the five-year program at the University of New Hampshire. For their papers students were asked "to consider their personal values, goals, and attributes and their recent semester of experience in teaching and to evaluate the possibility of teaching as a career." Preliminary analysis indicates the most important factor for those choosing to continue in the preservice program is "social service motivation," or wanting to make a contribution in an area of social need. The second most important factor is "enjoyment of children," and the third is "love of subject." According to the investigators, motivating factors for males and females differ, but the analysis is unclear regarding in what ways.

Bontempo and Digman surveyed entry-level education undergraduates at West Virginia University. Reasons for choosing teaching as a career by percentage are: enjoyment of working with children (50%), desire to help others learn (26%), interest in subject matter (20%), and the act of teaching itself (14%). The investigators note that 59% of the female subjects compared with 37% of the males are confident about their choice of teaching as a career.

Book and Freeman compared differences between 174 elementary and 178 secondary entry-level education majors at Michigan State University. Among the results reported are that elementary majors are more likely to choose teaching because of their interest in children, while the secondary majors choose teaching because of their subject matter interests.

Book, Freeman, and Brousseau determined reasons why education majors choose teaching and compared them with reasons non-education majors choose other fields of study. Subjects were 258 education majors and 146 non-education majors. The most common reasons education majors choose to teach are listed below by percentages:

"Through this career I can help others gain a sense of personal achievement and self esteem." (95%)

"I love to work with children." (81%)

"Through this career I can help others gain knowledge and understanding of things I consider important." (79%)

"I can make better use of my abilities in this field." (75%)

"This career provides an opportunity to apply what I have learned in my major field of study." (63%)

"This career provides an opportunity to help others less fortunate than myself." (53%)

By contrast, non-education majors choose their careers for the most part because:

"I can make better use of my abilities." (80%)

"This career provides an opportunity to apply what I have learned in my major field of study." (75%)

"Salaries are at least adequate." (67%)

Horton, Daniel, and Summers at Indiana State University compared reasons for choosing teaching as a career as expressed by secondary majors a decade apart (1971-73 and 1982-83). Among other findings, these investigators concluded that the more recent group was more concerned for people (48% compared to 19%), less concerned with job security (2.1% compared to 6.6%), and less influenced by former teachers they had had (6.2% compared to 14.6%).

Jantzen investigated the reasons for choosing teaching as a career in California from 1946 until 1979. Over the years he administered a 16-item questionnaire listing "attractors" to teaching to presumably convenience samples of preservice teachers. Jantzen reports significant shifts in the reasons for choosing teaching over time. For example, in 1979, 95% of females chose to teach because of special interest in young people, compared to 80% reporting this reason in 1949. Among males, 95% chose to teach because it "offers a reasonable assurance of an adequate income," compared to 68% reporting this reason in 1946. Other high-ranking attractors include "Teaching offers a lifelong opportunity to learn" (females 71%, males 67%), "Teaching gives me an opportunity to exercise individual initiative" (females 61%, males 66%), and "Enthusiasm of some former teacher" (females 58%, males 61%). By contrast, some attractors are reported less frequently over time. For example, the attraction of a long summer vacation is down for both males and females, and assurance of an adequate income is way down for females (only 24% in 1979 compared to 88% in 1951).

Joseph and Green asked 234 preservice teachers at a predominantly commuter college to respond to statements of reasons for choosing teaching as a career. The most common reasons selected were: desire to work with people, to be of service, and to have a career that is absorbing and allows for creativity (all more than 90%); desire to continue to be in a school setting (79%); teaching is time compatible and allows for vacations (48%); and teaching has material benefits and is something to fall back on (34%).

Kemper and Mangieri studied the interest in teaching of college-bound high school students and identified correlates of such interest. They administered questionnaires to 4,349 juniors and seniors in urban, suburban, and rural settings in seven states. The 35% who indicated they were either "very" or "somewhat interested" in a teaching career reported three major factors related to that interest: knowledge and skill in the subject they would teach (76%), interest in the subject they would teach (68%), and desire to work with children or young adults (64%). Notable were some of the sex differences among high school students interested in teaching. For example, job security was rated more important by females (62% compared to 40% for males) as was desire to work with children (73% compared to 50% for males). Also, females were more often influenced by a person who taught (45% compared to 14% for males).

The Research About Teacher Education Project used a sample of 876 preservice teachers selected from 76 member institutions of the American Association of Colleges for Teacher Education. The subjects reported the following reasons for choosing teaching as a career: helping children grow and learn (90%), a challenging field (63%), work opportunities and conditions of employment (54%), inspired by a teacher (53%), view teaching as an honorable vocation (52%), offers career-related opportunities (44%), able to be admitted to the program (41%), reputation of education on campus (22%), and friends in the school of education (20%).

Roberson, Keith, and Page, using the 1980 Longitudinal Study data (Riccobono et al. 1981), identified 688 high school seniors who intended to become K-12 teachers. Then they used a path model to describe relationships between and among 18 variables related to aspirations to teaching as a career. Findings indicate that high school seniors desiring to teach are best described as being female, having a desire to work with people, and having been influenced to teach by former teachers. When compared with pupils from the same population not intending to teach, they are less concerned with income and job security.

Wood used a sample of 52 education majors at the State University of New York, Old Westbury College and asked them to respond to the query, "What prompted you to become a teacher?" The 73 responses (some provided multiple reasons) fell into eight categories as follows: personal experience with children (33%), liking children (27%), altruistic reasons (16%), influence of a relative (8%), respond to unjust criticisms of schools (6%), job advantages (4%), influence of a former teacher (3%), and liking for school and learning (3%).

When Yarger, Howey, and Joyce asked 2,200 preservice teachers their reasons for choosing teaching as a career, the overwhelming reason given was desire to work with children. Other influential factors seem to be working hours, vacations, and security. Although respondents saw teaching as fulfilling, important, and challenging, they did not see it as having power or status.

Table 8 (p. 96) provides a rough extrapolation across studies of the reasons college-bound high school students and preservice teachers give for choosing teaching as a career. It should be noted that the investigators used different population samples and different data collection techniques.

Why Do Persons Choose Not to Teach?

This question is addressed somewhat by Andrew (1983); Book, Freeman, and Brousseau (1985); Kemper and Mangieri (1985); and Nutter (1983).

Andrew found that students undecided about whether to continue in the preservice program at the University of New Hampshire gave as their reasons: their own personal shortcomings (lack of confidence, lack of patience, not liking children), low salaries, extra duties, and experience with poor models (apathetic and lazy teachers). The preservice teachers who actually quit the program reported they did so because of personal shortcomings, concern about discipline-related problems, extra duties, low salary, and monotony.

Book, Freeman, and Brousseau in their study comparing education majors and non-education majors cite the following reasons for not considering a career in teaching: inadequate salaries, lack of job security, limited opportunities for advancement, monotony and boredom, little satisfaction or challenge, and lack of flexibility.

In the Kemper and Mangieri study of high school students, the subjects identified as having either no interest in teaching or no opinion one way or the other reported that their reluctance to consider teaching as a career was for the following reasons: low salaries, the need for more rapid salary advancement than teaching permits, and greater opportunities in other fields.

Nutter conducted a study at Ohio University to determine why preservice teachers drop out of the program. Her study used a questionnaire administered to a convenience sample of 42 program leavers. The reasons given for leaving the teacher preparation program in order of frequency were: greater interest in another field (82%), lack of job opportunities (71%), low salaries (56%), lack of job security (38%), the low status of teaching (23%), and concerns about school discipline (21%).

From the studies reviewed above, a composite list of reasons for deciding not to enter a teacher preparation program or for dropping out of a program include the following:

Table 8. Reasons given most often by college-bound and preservice teachers for choosing a teaching career.

Reported by

Reasons	Andrew	Bontempo & Digman	Book & Freeman	Book, Freeman & Brousseau	Jantzen	Joseph & Green	Kamper & Mangieri	Research About etc.	Roberson et al.	Wood	Yarger et al.
I have a social service (people) orientation	X		X		X			X	X	X	
I am interested in and enjoy children	X	X	X	X	X		X	X		X	X
I love an academic subject	X	X	X					X			
I want to help others learn		X		X				X			
I enjoy teaching		X									
I can use subject matter I know		X					X				
I have teaching ability		X									
I find income from teaching adequate						X	X				
I enjoy being associated with learning and schools						X	X			X	
I can use my individuality, initiative, creativity						X	X				
I was influenced by significant others						X		X	X	X	
I enjoy the hours and vacations						X	X	X		X	X
I find schools to be unjustly criticized									X		
I think teaching is challenging/important								X			X
I think teaching could lead to another career								X			

- perceived personal shortcomings that would seem to be detrimental for successful teaching
- inadequate salaries
- extra duties
- perception of teachers as apathetic, lazy
- concern about school discipline
- monotony and boredom
- lack of job security
- limited opportunity for advancement
- little satisfaction or challenge
- lack of flexibility
- interest in another field
- low status of teachers

How Long Do Preservice Teachers Expect to Teach?

A few investigators have sampled the views of preservice teachers as to how long they expect to stay in teaching. They include Bontempo and Digman (1985); Book, Byers, and Freeman (1983); Book and Freeman (1986); Research About Teacher Education Project (1987); and Sharp and Hirshfeld (1975).

According to Bontempo and Digman, females in preservice education express a greater commitment to teaching than do males (59% female, 37% male). Most of their subjects perceived themselves as remaining in the classroom or in education-related jobs throughout their careers; 51% saw themselves as professionally active beyond age 65.

Similarly, Book, Byers, and Freeman report that their subjects felt they would remain in teaching. Of their sample of 473 freshmen and sophomores enrolled in two entry-level education courses at Michigan State University during 1981-82, 57% planned to teach 10 or more years. Of those preservice teachers who expected to leave teaching, 25% would do so to continue their education, 42% to raise a family, and 21% to change careers. Female preservice teachers whose mothers were not employed outside the home were especially prone to report that they would leave teaching to raise a family.

Book and Freeman, using a sample of 174 elementary and 178 secondary preservice teachers at Michigan State University, found that upon entering the teacher preparation program, elementary majors were more committed to teaching than were secondary majors. Of the elementary majors, 38% reported that teaching was the only career considered compared to 23% of the secondary majors. Also, only 13% of the elementary majors anticipated leaving teaching for other careers compared to 48% of the secondary majors.

According to the Research About Teacher Education Project, students enrolled in teacher education programs view themselves as preparing for long-term careers in the classroom, with nearly half believing their careers will span 10 years or more.

In the Sharp and Hirshfeld study examining the projected career plans of college freshmen in 1967 and then their actual first occupational choices on graduation in 1971, it was found that the career goals of students entering education generally were more stable than those of students who indicated early interest in other fields, and that 40% of the education majors planned to teach most of their lives.

What Are the Backgrounds of Preservice Teachers?

Several investigators have studied the demographic characteristics of teacher education majors. They include Book, Byers, and Freeman (1983); Book and Freeman (1986); Book, Freeman, and Brousseau (1985); Galluzzo and Arends (1989); Joyce et al. (1977); Research About Teacher Education Project (1987), Roberson, Keith, and Page (1983); Sharp and Hirshfeld (1975); and Yarger, Howey, and Joyce (1977).

Book, Byers, and Freeman identified the following major demographic characteristics in their sample of preservice teachers: 94% Caucasian, 79% female, 88% educated in public high schools, 52% graduating in classes with more than 300, most received their K-12 education in the same school district, and 80% had experience in working with youth.

Book and Freeman report that the background and experience of their sample of elementary education majors differ from the secondary majors in the following ways: weaker in science and math, much more likely to take remedial math in college, more likely to have worked with children in both school and non-school settings and to have worked with handicapped youth, and more likely to have graduated from smaller high schools. In the total sample of both elementary and secondary majors, females are more likely to have studied three or more years of foreign language in high school.

Book, Freeman, and Brousseau found a majority of their sample of preservice teachers at Michigan State University to be female, Caucasian, to come from relatively large families (53% from families with four or more children), to come from families in which both parents have earned some college credits (57% of mothers and 67% of fathers), and to have experience working with children. Additionally, they read for pleasure. Compared to non-education majors, they are less likely to come from higher income families.

Joyce et al. surveyed 2,200 preservice teachers from 175 teacher-preparing institutions. The demographics of their sample are as follows: 75% under age 25, 30% married, 67% female, 87% Caucasian, 83% graduating from public high schools, 31% having fathers who were self-employed or professionals, and 36% having homemaker mothers.

The Research About Teacher Education Project (RATE) reported the following demographic characteristics for its sample of 876 secondary preservice teachers: Slightly more than three-quarters are female, 89% are Caucasian, and 25% are married. At graduation their average age is 24 to 25. About 10% have an average age of 34 and are receiving their first degree in education as post-baccalaureate students. Almost half are commuters, and 40% are transfer students. About one-half attend college within 50 miles of their homes, which are located in suburban or rural communities. Three-fourths report outside employment. Very few report foreign language fluency.

Galluzzo and Arends (1989) in a later release of RATE data conclude that white females constitute about two-thirds of all teaching majors and white males about one-quarter.

Roberson, Keith, and Page, as do Joyce et al., report the majority of high school students intending to become teachers are female.

The Sharp and Hirshfeld study, involving education majors enrolled between 1967-71, reports the following demographic characteristics: 80% of those graduating are female, 70% of their fathers and 80% of their mothers have a high school education, and most receive their teacher preparation in small to medium-size, four-year colleges. Further, 80% receive parental financial support, 56% are employed while in school, and 26% have federal student loans.

Yarger, Howey, and Joyce, using the same data source as Joyce et al., conclude that the typical preservice teacher is female, Caucasian, comes from a small city or rural area, is monolingual, and attends college in her native state, usually near home.

What Personal Characteristics Distinguish Preservice Teachers?

Numerous investigations of preservice teachers have studied their personal attributes, such as academic and intellectual abilities, confidence and adjustment, attitudes and values, and preferences. Among these studies are: Bontempo and Digman (1985); Book, Byers, and Freeman (1983); Book and Freeman (1986); Book, Freeman, and Brousseau (1985); Borko, Lalik, and Tomchin (1987); Callahan (1980); Carnegie Foundation (1986); Cooperman and Klagholz (1985); Domas and Tiedeman (1950); Dravland

and Greene (1980); Dupois (1984); Fisher and Feldman (1985); Frank (1986); Gallegos and Gibson (1982); Guyton and Forokhi (1985); Henjum (1969); Matczynski et al. (1988); Nelli (1984); Nelson (1985); Olsen (1985); Phillips (1982); Pigge (1985); Pigge and Marso (1987); Research About Teacher Education Project (1987); Richardson and Briggs (1983); Roberson, Keith, and Page (1983); Savage (1983); Sharp and Hirshfeld (1975); Skipper and Quantz (1987); Stolee (1982); Vance and Schlechty (1982); Weaver (1979); and Yarger, Howey, and Joyce (1977).

Studies of academic ability. Two distinctly different bodies of literature exist for this topic. One group of studies compares actual preservice teachers with non-education majors. The other compares high school students who say they *intend* to major in education in college with high school students who state they intend to major in areas other than education. The first group of studies summarized below deals with preservice teachers.

Barger and Barger, reported in Matczynski et al. (1988), compared 3,831 education and non-education students at Eastern Illinois University on the following criteria: ACT scores, high school class rank, cumulative grade point average, and grade point average in their upper division major. They report the following findings: The mean cumulative grade point average for education majors was 3.09 compared to 2.96 for non-education majors; the mean upper division grade point average for education majors was 3.19 and for non-education majors 3.15. Education majors were slightly lower in composite ACT scores and high school class rank.

At Michigan State University, Book, Freeman, and Brousseau also compared the academic backgrounds of education and non-education majors. The two groups compared were 258 students enrolled in an introductory educational psychology class, who indicated either that teaching was their only career consideration or that it was first choice on a list of career options, and 146 students enrolled in an introductory communications course. Comparison of the academic backgrounds of the two groups revealed the high school academic preparation of members of the two groups to be similar. Their high school grade point averages were very close (3.14 for education majors, 3.07 for non-education majors). About equal numbers from both groups were judged deficient enough to require remedial courses in college. Education majors were more likely to read for pleasure and more likely to have been elected to the National Honor Society.

Cohen, reported in Matczynski et al. (1988), compared large numbers of education and non-education students from 18 campuses of the California State University system on the following criteria: cumulative grade point average, grade point average in their majors, grade point average at the beginning of professional education courses, and grade point average in basic skills courses. On all grade point criteria, the education majors achieved at or above the mean of non-education majors.

Dravland and Greene found education majors had higher grade point averages and a higher program completion rate than did non-education majors.

Dupois studied sophomores and juniors who had completed most of their general education requirements and were beginning professional courses at six large and small Pennsylvania institutions. When compared with non-education sophomores, she found them to be close to the level of reading skills expected of sophomores in Pennsylvania and in the top half of college students nationwide. Nearly a quarter scored above the level of a college senior in reading, while only four percent had scores low enough to indicate a significant problem. Within professional education, elementary majors consistently outperformed secondary majors in study habits and attitudes.

Fisher and Feldman compared the academic ability of 2,100 education majors and 6,700 non-education students at Illinois State University between 1980-83. Criteria for comparison included ACT scores, cumulative grade point averages, and cumulative grade point averages for general studies and for upper division courses. Education majors compared favorably on all measures.

Guyton and Forokhi used a sample of 782 students from the three largest colleges (arts and sciences, business, and education) at Georgia State University and compared the students from the three colleges on several measures. With regard to grade point averages, at the sophomore level arts and science majors had the highest GPA's (3.01), followed by education majors (2.88), and business majors (2.60). Final GPA's upon graduation showed education majors to have the highest (3.3), followed by arts and science (3.12), and business (2.72). Scores on the State Regents Test showed negligible differences among the three groups.

Matczynski et al. compared education majors with majors in arts and sciences, business, communication and computer science, library science, and nursing graduating from Clarion University in 1984-85. One comparison criterion was the mean grade point averages on 13 required general education courses. Grade point averages for the non-education majors were as follows: arts and science (2.70), business (2.62), communication and computer science (2.69), library science (2.30), and nursing (3.59). The mean grade point average for education majors in the same general education courses was 2.78, thus placing them in second place behind nursing majors. Additionally, the investigators compared arts and science majors

101

with secondary education majors in courses they took in common, that is, the courses the secondary education majors took for their teaching major, such as biology, chemistry, physics, earth science, English, and mathematics. Grade points earned in common courses by secondary education majors compared with arts and science majors were as follows (the secondary education majors' grade points are given first): biology 2.81 and 2.74, chemistry 2.83 and 2.71, English 3.0 and 2.72, earth science 3.37 and 2.54, math 2.34 and 2.97, and physics 3.0 and 2.01.

Similarly, Nelli compared grade point averages of secondary education majors and non-education majors at the University of Kentucky in courses taken in common (natural sciences, mathematics, foreign language, music, social sciences, English, or art). It was found that secondary education majors received grades equal to those received by the non-education majors.

Nelson used the National Longitudinal Study (NLS) data (see Riccobono et al. 1981) of the high school class of 1972 to find out how those who entered teaching after college compared to those who chose different careers. The measures used to make the comparisons included SAT, ACT, and NLS test scores and high school class rank. His findings showed that non-teachers outscored teachers on the following: SAT-verbal 489 to 459, SAT-math 528 to 486, ACT-English 20.1 to 19.7, ACT-math 22.6 to 20.1, NLS vocabulary 5.27 to 5.07, NLS math 5.37 to 5.15, and class rank 69.5 to 68.8. By contrast, teachers outscored non-teachers on the NLS reading test 5.01 to 4.98.

At the University of Wisconsin-Parkside, Olsen compared 107 education majors with 1,420 non-education majors. Both groups had completed their baccalaureate degree. On 11 variables, three statistically significant differences were found and all favored education majors. They had higher high school percentile ranks (taken from student transcripts), higher cumulative university grade point averages, and higher grades in a common university course (English 101).

The Research About Teacher Education Project reached the following conclusions relative to the academic achievement of education majors. Preservice teachers have about the same ability as the general undergraduate population and upon graduation have a cumulative grade point average of around 3.0. They receive slightly higher marks in their education courses than in non-education courses. The typical teacher education student is in the top third of his or her high school class and falls in the average range on SAT math and verbal tests.

Savage studied the academic qualifications of women choosing education as a career compared with women choosing other fields of study. The sample included 1,081 women in seven fields of study who were followed over four years of college. Of the seven fields, women in education ranked sixth on SAT scores and tied for last place in high school class ranking. Women transferring into education had both higher SAT scores and higher class rank than the mean of education majors.

Sharp and Hirshfeld report that the subjects in their study (college freshmen in 1967 who declared their intent to pursue a career in teaching and upon graduation took teaching positions) when compared with "defector" subjects who changed career goals to another field, were less likely to have scored high and more likely to have scored low on an academic index. Relatedly, subjects who scored high on the academic index indicated the shortest commitment to teaching as a career.

Stolee analyzed data on freshmen entering the University of Wisconsin-Milwaukee during 1980-1981. He concluded from these data that both the high school percentile rank and SAT scores for the prospective education majors were higher than those of the non-education majors. Additionally, he reports that graduating education majors had higher overall grade point averages and that their grades in courses outside of education were higher with one exception (allied health).

The next set of studies reviewed compares the academic ability of high school students who declare their intent to major in education with those who do not.

Cooperman and Klagholz report that the 1982 SAT scores of New Jersey high school graduates who planned to major in education were lower than those of their peers planning to major in 22 of 24 fields. Furthermore, 60% of high school seniors who indicated interest in teaching and who were admitted to New Jersey community and state colleges scored 399 or lower on the verbal portion of the SAT compared to the statewide average of 416.

Roberson, Keith, and Page conclude that, "[I]t appears that teaching aspirants . . . are somewhat less able intellectually than their classmates" and that "lower ability is a notable influence [more characteristic of] females and blacks who aspire to teach, but not for white males" (p. 20). However, according to *Teacher Education Reports* (22 September 1988), the SAT scores of high school students aspiring to become teachers "has risen dramatically in recent years" (p. 4). It goes on to quote the co-author of the College Board's annual *Profiles, College-Bound Seniors*: "In 1988, they are much higher than at any year since we started tallying these particular data." Verbal scores were 11 points higher than in 1978 and mathematics scores were 20 points higher than in 1987. *Teacher Education Reports* concludes that the SAT gap between students stating they will major in education and students stating non-education majors is the smallest since Educational Testing Service began such data collection. The latest combined SAT scores for education majors is 849 compared to 904 for non-education majors.

Vance and Schlecty, as others, analyzed data from the National Longitudinal Study of 1,972 high school seniors. They compared seniors who later completed college (although not necessarily as education majors) and entered teaching with non-education majors who entered other careers. On the basis of their analysis of SAT scores, the investigators conclude that teaching is more attractive to individuals with lower academic ability but that education does attract and retain a proportional share of those in the middle range of academic ability.

Weaver's study (probably the most quoted and creating the most controversy) compared the academic qualifications of college-bound high school seniors who *aspired* to teach with those who planned other careers. On the SAT, those aspiring to teach scored 34 points lower on the verbal portion and 43 points lower on the mathematics portion. Overall, high school seniors planning to study education had lower scores as a group than seniors planning to major in the six other majors (business administration and commerce, biological sciences, engineering fields, health and medical fields, physical sciences, and social sciences). The investigator notes that ACT data show essentially the same thing. Of 19 fields of study reported by ACT for college freshmen in 1975-76, education majors were in 14th place in English and tied for 17th place in math. For high school seniors participating in the National Longitudinal Study (NLS), those intending to become education majors ranked 14th and 15th out of 16 fields on SAT scores and ranked 12th on grade point averages. Further, these aspiring education majors were below the mean of all high school seniors on the NLS tests in vocabulary, reading, and math. Another bit of depressing news from the Weaver study was the finding that an NLS sub-sample of education majors graduating in 1976 who did not find or did not take teaching jobs was, for the most part, more academically able!

In a related but somewhat different genre of studies, Gallegos and Gibson compared academic characteristics of education students graduating from Western Washington University in 1969-71 with those graduating in 1979-81 and found the latter group superior to those a decade earlier on cumulative grade point average, even though the median GPA at that institution had declined over the 10-year interval.

Pigge compared the academic qualifications of teacher education graduates who become full-time teachers with those of teacher education graduates who did not take teaching jobs (somewhat similar to the Weaver sub-sample described above). A questionnaire was mailed to 3,061 graduates from the college of education of a medium-sized Ohio university between 1980-83. Of the more than 1,000 respondents, 55% became full-time teachers within three months of graduation, 14% became substitute teachers, 12% could not find teaching jobs, and 19% chose other fields of work. After comparing such things as high school class rank, university grade point averages, and ACT scores, Pigge concludes that the most academically able do not choose to embark on teaching careers. Rather, they either continue their education or enter other fields of employment. The least academically able were those who could not find teaching jobs and those who were substitute teachers.

A summary of the above studies comparing the academic ability of education majors with non-education majors follows. During high school, prospective education majors in one study had about the same grade point average as other students who went on to college; in two studies they had a higher class rank; in two other studies a slightly lower class rank, and in another study a lower class rank. In one study they were more often members of the National Honorary Society. In one study they had about the same scores on State Regents Tests. In one study they had the same ACT scores and in another slightly lower scores. In one study they had higher SAT scores and in another lower scores. In one study they had lower scores on National Longitudinal Studies Tests.

During college, education majors in two studies were no more likely to require remedial work. In one study they had the same reading ability and in another slightly higher reading ability. In one study they received higher grades in introductory English. In three studies they received the same grades in their academic majors. In one study they read more for recreation. In one study they had a slightly higher grade point average in general studies and, in another, the same grade point average in general studies. In two studies they had the same upper division grade point average. In two studies they had a higher cumulative grade point average and in three studies the same cumulative grade point average.

Personality characteristics of preservice teachers. Book, Byers, and Freeman found that lower division education majors were generally confident in their ability to teach, with 24% expressing complete confidence and 66% being moderately confident.

Callahan queried 120 elementary and secondary preservice teachers at Washington State University. He found preservice teachers to be confident before student teaching and even more so after that experience. He also found that they possessed many of the attributes of good teachers ("friendly, knowledgeable and poised, lively and interesting, firm control, and democratic").

Dumas and Tiedeman cite studies comparing education majors and non-education majors that find no significant differences with regard to personality.

Dravland and Greene report in their study that education majors were more submissive when compared with non-educaton majors. Also, male education majors were more conscientious, group dependent, and had higher self-concepts when compared with male non-education majors.

Using a sample of 78 student teachers at the University of Minnesota, Henjum studied the relationship between certain personality characteristics of secondary student teachers and their success in that role as perceived by their pupils and supervisors. He conducted correlational analysis and analysis of variance of student teachers' responses to Cattel's *Sixteen Personality Form Questionnaire*, pupils' responses on the Hoyt-Grim *Pupil Reaction Inventory*, and the university supervisor's assigned letter grades and rankings of the student teachers. Among the findings are: In order to be perceived as successful at the senior high level, it is important for student teachers to be "highly intelligent and enthusiastic"; and at the junior high level, they should be "emotionally mature, experimenting, somewhat extroverted, and socially adjusted."

Richardson and Briggs asked cooperating teachers to describe the attributes of secondary student teachers at East Texas State University by using a 31-item semantic differential scale. On a five-point scale, the student teachers were perceived to be courteous (4.64), cooperative and trusting (4.56), friendly (4.53), good-natured (4.51), sincere and kind (4.46). In fact, the means for each of the 31 personal attributes was 3.61 or above, indicating that cooperating teachers generally found these student teachers personally acceptable.

Attitudes, values, perceptions. Bontempo and Digman found undergraduates entering teacher preparation to view teaching as important (43%), rewarding (39%), underrated (28%), and difficult (12%).

Pigge and Marso investigated relationships between characteristics of beginning education majors at a medium-sized Ohio university and their attitudes, anxieties, and confidence level about teaching. Among their many findings are: elementary majors have a more positive attitude toward teaching; those deciding to teach early-on have more positive attitudes toward teaching; respondents are most anxious about finding teaching satisfying, having pupils follow their directions, preparing lessons, and having the ability to control a class; respondents were least anxious about being happy with teaching, differences in backgrounds between themselves and their pupils, answering pupil questions, lack of pupil rapport; their major concerns were lack of instructional materials and meeting the needs of different pupils; and they had minimal concern about having too many non-instructional duties, having too many pupils, routine, and the inflexible nature of teaching.

The Research About Teacher Education Project examined the attitudes of preservice secondary teachers toward teaching as a career and found the vast majority to have positive or very positive attitudes.

Skipper and Quantz studied changes in the attitudes of 45 education majors and 63 arts and science majors at Miami University by administering an attitude survey to freshmen in 1980 and again to the same students when they were seniors in 1984. Comparisons within and across the two groups resulted in the following findings: as freshmen, education majors were significantly less progressive regarding educational practices than arts and science majors; as seniors, both groups became more progressive but with the greater change occurring among education majors. Education majors were more progressive with regard to professional issues, such as supporting academic freedom for teachers and viewing teachers as experts on teaching and learning, while arts and science majors were more progressive with regard to teaching democracy and criticizing our political and economic system.

Book, Byers, and Freeman, in their study of preservice teachers' attitudes toward teacher preparation, report that their sample expressed as an overriding belief that experience is the best teacher. Their subjects expected "on-the-job training and supervised teaching experiences to be the most valuable sources of professional knowledge" (p. 10). They also report that elementary majors mostly value coursework in educational psychology and instructional methods.

Callahan found that elementary and secondary education majors value teacher characteristics that researchers have determined to be desirable. These include knowledge, poise, friendliness, being lively and interesting, having firm control, and using democratic procedures. However, they perceive their preparation programs as only marginally contributing to their attaining these characteristics.

A Carnegie study based on national surveys of college students in 1975 and 1984 reported that: education majors were pleased with the teaching and education they receive; they were less inclined to feel they are treated like "numbers in a book"; they reported greater interaction with their professors; they felt there were faculty to whom they could turn; they felt faculty

107

took special interest in them; and they trusted professors to look out for their interests. More so than students in other majors except perhaps engineering, those intending to have long careers as teachers want a "detailed grasp of [their] specialized field." Clearly, they want "training and skills" for their occupation.

Yarger, Howey, and Joyce report that their subjects felt competent in classroom management, in teaching their specialty, and in their ability to relate to colleagues. They felt the need for additional preparation in diagnosis and remediation of learning problems and in using human and material resources. Other perceived shortcomings in their professional courses related to lack of preparation in classroom management and in multicultural education.

Regarding teaching goals as perceived by preservice teachers, Bontempo and Digman indicate that the most mentioned are motivating pupils to learn (34%) and preparing pupils for the world (26%). Book, Byers, and Freeman report that their subjects' major teaching goals are enhancing pupil self-image (46%) and promoting academic achievement (31%).

To determine student teachers' perception of what constitutes a successful lesson, Borko examined the journals kept by 26 elementary student teachers from a Southeastern university. The journals of seven stronger and seven weaker students were examined to see if there were differences in perceptions of successful lessons. Both stronger and weaker students shared similar perceptions that successful lessons were characterized as having instructional uniqueness or creativity, good organization and time management, appropriate pacing, effective grouping for instruction, adequate planning and preparation, proper pupil management or control, and appropriate outcomes in terms of pupil learning and satisfaction.

Preferences. Regarding where they wished to teach, Book, Byers, and Freeman report a preference by 66% of preservice teachers from suburban and rural areas to return to those settings. By contrast, only 25% of preservice teachers from urban areas indicated a preference to teach in such areas. They more often express interest in teaching in suburban schools (29%) or have no preference (33%). Caucasian students more than nonwhites prefer suburban teaching; few (6%) indicate interest in an urban teaching position. Another finding was that 75% percent would prefer to teach within the state. The Research About Teacher Education Project also looked into geographic teaching preferences and found that 75% of preservice teachers would prefer to remain within 100 miles of their home communities and that 82% prefer teaching in rural or suburban areas.

Phillips, in a study of the learning style preferences of Ohio State University preservice teachers, reports that 65% of her subjects like "hands-on" experiences and that females express a stronger preference than do males. Skipper and Quantz also surveyed preservice teachers at Miami University regarding preferred learning styles and found differences between elementary and secondary preservice teachers. Elementary preservice teachers prefer to learn in a group situation, place a higher priority on well-organized courses that stay on schedule, and prefer not to give oral reports.

Regarding cognitive style, Frank found female education students with teaching majors in sciences, mathematics, business, and physical education to be more task-oriented and analytical, whereas students with teaching majors in social science, humanities, family and child development, home economics, special education, and speech pathology tended to be more socially oriented and to be global processors of information.

Summary of Research on the Preservice Teacher

Extrapolating from the studies on preservice teachers reviewed above, the following tentative generalizations can be made.

Persons who decide to teach do so mainly because of their social service orientation and their liking for children. Additionally, they do so because of positive job-related factors, such as school hours and vacations and a liking for an academic subject. On the other hand, persons who drop out of preservice programs do so because they perceive they have personal shortcomings; they don't like the extra duties and low salaries; and they perceive teaching to be monotonous.

Females and elementary majors are more likely to express a long-term commitment to teaching. Overall, about half of those in preservice programs intend at least a 10-year stint in K-12 classrooms.

Preservice teachers can be characterized mostly as Caucasian females who have had prior experiences with children. They are graduates of suburban and rural public schools. They come from larger families, like to read, and are rarely fluent in a foreign language. They are educated in small to medium-sized universities near home and are place-bound in their choice of where they wish to teach.

Compared with non-education majors, preservice teachers are equal on the usual measures of academic achievement such as grade point average in high school and college but do less well on standard tests of academic aptitude.

Regarding personal qualities, preservice teachers are positive about teaching as a career, confident in their ability to teach, and are somewhat more submissive and less progressive. They are anxious mostly about whether teaching will be satisfying and whether they can handle pupils. They regard on-the-job training and coursework related to pedagogy as most valuable, and they respect the professional preparation they have received. Their goals are to enhance pupils' self-image and academic learning. They hope to teach in suburban or rural schools near their homes.

Preservice Curriculum and Instruction

Curriculum and instruction constitute different variables in the research on teacher education, although at times they overlap as in student teaching, a subset of the teacher preparation curriculum. In the following review of research, curriculum and instruction will be presented together.

Preservice Teacher Preparation Curriculum

Although the preservice teacher preparation curriculum is often talked about, most of what is said about it can best be described as conventional wisdom or expressions of opinion on what is commonly believed to be true. The review by Lanier and Little (1986), for example, is replete with assertions made with great confidence by stakeholders but without supporting data to back them up. Among the assertions made about the teacher preparation curriculum are that: course content is unstable and tends to reflect the personal ideology of the instructor; coursework is not intellectually rigorous; curricula are heavy with experiences that reinforce conservative and present-oriented approaches; preservice teachers are taught to think narrowly about the scope of their work; field experiences promote trial-and-error learning and an apprenticeship approach; recent research on teaching effectiveness is conceptualized narrowly, is presented as truth, and denies teacher wisdom; and general education is neglected.

Lanier and Little are able to identify few, if any, substantive studies of the teacher preparation curriculum. At one point they admit, "existing data do not allow clear portraits of the explicit teacher preparation curriculum to be drawn" (p. 548).

Koehler (1985) also was frustrated in her efforts to aggregate research on the comparative merits of teacher education curricula. Her ERIC search (circa 1980-84) proved to be mostly sterile with regard to significant findings. A large number of studies she found and reviewed were not comparative studies but rather were evaluations of one course or method using pre- and post-testing or just post-testing. She did identify comparative studies wherein the comparison groups receive different content treatment in a course. Although most of these studies found differences in treatment effects (one treatment was superior to another), Koehler notes that "none of the studies involved long-term follow-up of the [preservice] students into

110

classroom teaching, nor did they include descriptive research on the treatments themselves" (p. 24). Medley (1982) offers the same criticism of such program evaluation studies, because they fail to take into account program validation or whether the program's treatment effect makes a difference in preservice teachers' behavior once they take postions in K-12 classrooms.

Evertson, Hawley, and Zlotnick (1985) searched for studies that address the question: Do preservice preparation programs teach teachers to teach effectively? They identifed two groups of studies. The first group compared the effectiveness of regularly certified teachers with provisionally certified teachers. They aggregated the results of 13 studies conducted between 1958 and 1984 and found that in 11 of them regularly certified teachers were judged more effective on the basis of pupil achievement gains and ratings of administrators or trained observers. However, the investigators caution that most of these studies do not control well for other influential variables, such as length of the teachers' classroom experience, intelligence, or general academic competence.

The second group of studies aggregated by Evertson, Hawley, and Zlotnick sought to determine whether specific instructional strategies learned by preservice teachers are subsequently reflected in their K-12 classroom performance. They note that "numerous studies show that particular efforts by education schools to structure preservice teacher learning have desired effects on [preservice teacher] behavior in the short-run" (p. 4). However, they report mixed findings as to whether the newly acquired abilities transfer to student teaching or to teaching in natural classrooms.

Evertson, Hawley, and Zlotnick also report studies on the relationship between preservice teachers' subject matter knowledge and their effectiveness. Here, they rely on the work of Druva and Anderson (1983), who conducted an extensive investigation analyzing 65 studies of science education. Druva and Anderson conclude:

1. There is a relationship between teacher preparation programs and what their graduates do as teachers. Science courses, education courses, and overall academic performance are positively associated with successful teaching.
2. The relationship between teacher training in science and cognitive student outcomes is progressively higher in higher level science courses.
3. The most striking overall characteristic of the results is the pattern of low correlations across a large number of other variables involved (p. 478).

However, Evertson, Hawley, and Zlotnick report that in other subject fields the relationship between teachers' subject matter knowledge and either teacher performance or pupil learning is not clear. They also report they could not find any evidence to support the premise that the general education curriculum helps to promote desirable teacher characteristics. With regard to pedagogical preparation, they cite considerable evidence that there is a "knowledge base that might be covered in the preparation of teachers" (p. 6), which, if properly structured, could be used in preparing preservice teachers to become effective in the classroom.

A few efforts have been made to determine the precise content of the preservice teacher preparation curriculum and state education department certification requirements (Dumas and Weible 1984; Howey, Yarger, and Joyce 1978; Ishler 1984; Ishler and Kay 1981; Kluender 1984; Research About Teacher Education Project 1987; Weible and Dumas 1982).

Howey, Yarger, and Joyce surveyed 175 teacher preparing institutions to determine content distribution requirements. They found the norm to be 61 semester hours in general studies, 35 in professional studies, and 18 in applied or clinical work.

Ishler surveyed 66 member institutions of the Association of Colleges and Schools of Education in State Universities and of Land Grant Colleges and Affiliated Private Universities. He found that elementary majors take an average of 51 semester hours in general education (range of 33-81); for secondary majors the average was 47 semester hours (range of 30-65). In the area of content specialization, elementary majors averaged 29 semester hours (range of 12-38); and secondary majors averaged 35 semester hours (range of 22-66). Elementary majors spent an average of 200 hours in field experience prior to student teaching, while secondary majors spent an average of 92 hours. Both elementary and secondary majors received an average of nine semester hours credit for student teaching.

In a related study, Ishler and Kay surveyed 550 teacher-preparing institutions to determine norms for early field experiences (pre-student teaching). Responses from 240 institutions indicate that 99% require early field experience involving from 100 to 160 clock hours. The instructional activities early experience students engaged in most frequently are observation (99%), tutoring (98%), periodic reporting on the field experiences (95%), non-instructional tasks (91%), operating media (86%), planning instruction (84%), and designing instructional materials (82%). Activities engaged in least are determining pupil grades (1%), participating in parent conferences (1%), teaching the whole class (2%), attending professional meetings (3%), team teaching (4%), and teaching mini-lessons (5%).

The Research About Teacher Education Project (RATE) surveyed 76 member institutions of the American Association of Colleges for Teacher Education to determine the curriculum distribution requirements of preservice teachers. This study reports that the average number of semester credit hours required for the baccalaureate is 135. However, secondary majors on average take 10 more credit hours than do elementary majors. Secondary majors take an average of 26 credit hours in education courses compared to an average of 50 semester hours for elementary majors. This includes an average of 10 semester hours for student teaching, which typically involves 12 full weeks in the schools.

Galluzzo and Arends (1989) in a later report of the results of the RATE Project provide additional related data. Elementary education requirements include: 58 credit hours in general studies, 42 in professional studies, 20 in an area of concentration or academic minors, and 12 in student teaching. Secondary education majors typically are required to take 54 hours in general studies, 34 in their teaching specialty, 20 in a minor, 7 in methods courses, 4 in foundations, and 12 in student teaching.

The RATE Project also investigated secondary majors' reactions to their teacher preparation curriculum. It reports that nearly 90% rate their courses as "important" or "extremely important." Secondary majors felt they were well prepared to use proper teaching methods, plan, evaluate pupil learning, and respond to pupil differences. On the other hand, they felt less prepared to use computers, handle misbehavior, develop curriculum, and diagnose learner needs. The majority (66%) consider their education courses as rigorous as their non-education courses.

Kluender reviewed university catalogues and their program descriptions to determine the content distribution requirements of the teacher preparation curriculum. He reports the majority of coursework taken by preservice teachers is comprised of general education and the teaching specialty. For elementary majors the programs are divided roughly as follows: general education (40%), other related requirements (14%), and professional studies (44%). For secondary majors, the distribution is general education (40%), teaching specialty (39%), and professional studies (21%). Within professional studies, curriculum and methods courses account for 21% for elementary majors and 6% for secondary majors. Foundations courses in education are also more prevalent for elementary majors (11%) compared to secondary majors (7%).

The major studies of state education department teacher certification requirements are those of Dumas and Weible (1984) and Weible and Dumas (1982). The 1984 Dumas and Weible study identified state requirements for elementary teacher certification in 46 states. Of the 34 states prescribing general education requirements, the breakdown is as follows: history/social studies (100%), science (88%), English/composition (82%), mathematics (79%), and oral communication (17%).

Specific coursework in professional studies required by number of states is shown in Table 9.

Table 9. Coursework in professional studies required by states for elementary teacher certification.

Area of Study	Number of states (N = 46)
Student teaching	41
Teaching of reading	41
Educational psychology/growth and development	38
General curriculum methods, materials	27
Social foundations	23
Teaching of health and physical education	21
Teaching of math	20
Teaching of English	20
Teaching of children's literature	20
Teaching of science	18
Teaching of social studies	17
Teaching of exceptionality	17
Teaching of art	14
Teaching of music	12
Educational measurement	11

In addition to the data in Table 9, ten or fewer states require work in the following areas: educational media/technology (10), early field experiences (10), classroom management and discipline (8), community/parent relations (7), and school organization/administration (5). Some states require specific courses to be taken while others allude to study in a broad area.

The 1982 Weible and Dumas study sought the same information from states for secondary teacher certification. Of the 45 states providing usable data, only 23 listed specific coursework requirements in general education, broken down as follows: history/social studies (100%), English composition (87%), natural sciences (77%), humanities (74%), mathematics (69%), and oral communications (30%).

Specific coursework requirements in professional studies are shown in Table 10 by number of states. Only 39 states provided specifications.

114

Table 10. Coursework in professional studies required by states for secondary teacher certification.

Area of Study	Number of states (N = 39)
Student teaching	39
Educational psychology	38
General teaching methods	29
Social foundations	27
Special teaching methods	23
Reading in content area	21
Tests and evaluation	15
Early field experiences	15
Teaching exceptionality	14
School organization/administration	12
Multicultural education	12
Educational media	9

Instruction in Teacher Preparation Programs

Lanier and Little did not include instruction in teacher education in their review of research. Neither did Koehler's survey of research on teacher education address instruction per se, although her category "course/program/method evaluation" would seem to be related to the topic. Nevertheless, several studies do exist on instructional alternatives used in teacher preparation programs. Some of the alternatives studied include behavior modification, demonstration teaching, heuristics or inquiry, interaction analysis and other forms of classroom observation, mastery learning, microteaching, protocols, reflective teaching, simulations, and directed field experiences.

Behavior modification. Research on the effectiveness of behavior modification in teacher preparation has been synthesized by Allen and Forman (1984). Individual studies have been conducted by Andrews (1970); Bowles and Nelson (1976); Brown, Montgomery, and Barclay (1969); Cooper, Thomson, and Baer (1970); Cossairt, Hall, and Hopkins (1973); Horton (1975); Johnson and Sloat (1980); Ringer (1973); Sloat, Tharp, and Gallimore (1977); Thomson and Cooper (1969); and Woolfolk and Woolfolk (1974).

Among the findings from these studies, most of which used inservice teachers as subjects, are: teachers can be taught to use the principles of behavior modificaton; teachers report that when they use the principles pupil behavior is more positive; teachers seem to need reinforcement in order to continue to use the principles; teachers tend to use the principles when

115

teaching in subject matter areas used during their training; and use of the principles is improved when teachers can practice them by role-playing and viewing videotape feedback of their performance.

Demonstration teaching (modeling). Lange (1971) studied whether preservice teachers' observation of a videotaped teacher demonstrating indirect verbal behavior during reading instruction would affect their subsequent student teaching behavior. His subjects were 40 randomly selected female student teachers. Half of them (experimental group) were shown the 20-minute videotape; the other half (control group) viewed a "neutral movie" on reading instruction. Following the treatments, all subjects prepared and taught a reading lesson to their elementary pupils. The experimental group demonstrated significantly more indirect verbal behavior than did the control group. Thus a single 20-minute videotape demonstration of indirect verbal behaviors produced significant amounts of the target behavior, making a case for the potential of modeling in teacher preparation.

Putnam (1985) studied the attitudes of preservice teachers toward use of demonstration teaching done by the university education faculty. Subjects were 50 preservice teachers enrolled in one of several alternative teacher preparation programs at Michigan State University. The subjects observed 10 faculty members present lessons to K-12 pupils live and on videotape. The subjects preferred viewing live rather than videotaped demonstration lessons. They also reported that the only limitation to their involvement was loss of some of their own instructional time with the pupils. Putnam (1987) also reviewed earlier research on using films to demonstrate teaching skills and concluded that "training programs incorporating demonstration are more effective than those which exclude it" (p. 578).

Heuristics or inquiry. The effectiveness of inquiry as an instructional method in teacher preparation programs has been studied by Cotten, Evans, and Tseng (1978); George and Nelson (1971); Hurst (1974); Lombard, Konicek, and Schultz (1985); Porterfield (1974); and Zevin (1973), among others. Those studies that examined efforts to teach mostly inservice teachers to use more inductive/inquiry approaches conclude that such instruction results in subjects using more higher-order and probing questions and fewer lower-order questions. It also was found that less experienced teachers are more likely to use more inquiry approaches and that modeling the target behaviors enhances their acquisition.

Interaction analysis. Interaction analysis took the teacher education world by storm in the 1960s. Its effectiveness has been studied by Bondi (1970); Flanders (1963), one of its inventors; Furst (1967); Hough and Amidon (1967); Hough, Lohman, and Ober (1969); Hough and Ober (1966); Kirk

(1967); Langer and Allen (1970); Lohman, Ober, and Hough (1967); Luebkemann (1965); and Sandefur, Pankratz and Couch (1967), among others. Most subjects in these studies were preservice teachers. Among the findings are that instruction in interaction analysis tends to increase use of indirect teacher influence (accepting pupils' feelings, praising and encouraging, accepting and using pupil ideas, and question asking). Conversely, such instruction tends to reduce use of direct teacher influence (lecturing, direction-giving, and criticism). Also, those who are more "indirect" prior to receiving instruction become even more so after receiving instruction; and those who receive instruction have more spontaneous pupil talk in their classrooms. Another finding is that knowledge of and skill in interaction analysis are associated with positive attitudes toward classroom observation by those who use it.

Mastery Learning. Research on the use of mastery learning (well-planned and executed instruction with adequate pacing and monitoring and immediate and corrective feedback) in preservice teacher preparation is reported by Clark, Guskey, and Bennings (1983) and Robin (1976). To determine the effectiveness of mastery learning, Clark, Guskey, and Bennings used a variation of it described as group- and teacher-paced, rather than individual and self-paced. Subjects were 197 education majors enrolled in six sections of a course in educational psychology. Two sections comprising 55 subjects (experimental group) were taught by instructors who volunteered to implement mastery learning. The other four sections (control group) were taught by instructors in their usual fashion. Pretests of all subjects indicated no differences between the experimental and control groups with regard to knowledge of educational psychology, self-perceived academic ability, and interest and attitude toward education. Following the experiment all subjects took a common final exam. The results indicated that "on the average, students in the mastery classes attained higher scores, received higher course grades and had fewer absences" (p. 212).

Robin reviewed 39 studies in which mastery learning approaches were compared with traditional approaches at the college level. It is assumed, but not determinable from the review, that some education majors were involved in one or more of the investigations. The studies investigated use of individual rather than group-based instruction. According to Robin, the aggregated findings indicate that individual-based instruction is superior to traditional instruction in that learners are more likely to achieve higher final examination scores, retain the content longer, have more favorable attitudes toward the course, and spend more out-of-class time studying. On the negative side, this instructional approach seems plagued by a relatively

117

high student withdrawal rate. Evidently, working alone and at one's own pace is not suited to certain university students.

Microteaching. Definitions of microteaching vary. Here, the original meaning is used: a laboratory teaching encounter wherein a preservice teacher demonstrates one of several specified technical skills of teaching (for example, set induction, stimulus variation) when teaching a short lesson to a small group of peers and receives feedback regarding his or her proficiency level in the target skill.

A large amount of research has been conducted on microteaching and is reviewed elsewhere (Copeland 1982; Macleod 1987*a* and *b*; Turney et al. 1973). Copeland reports the following generalizations regarding the use of microteaching. When preservice teachers are to learn a technical skill, they should first have an example demonstrated for them. Use of peers as learners is adequate for the initial practice of a skill, but practicing the skill with K-12 pupils is more useful in transferring the skill to a natural classroom. The provision of feedback regarding level of skill proficiency is important, but no feedback mechanism (videotape versus audiotape) has been shown to be superior. The presence of a supervisor enhances skill learning.

Copeland also reports the following generalizations regarding the evaluation of microteaching. The process does increase initial acquisition of the targeted technical skills. Preservice teachers will more likely use the skills learned through microteaching when, as student teachers, their cooperating teachers demonstrate such skills or encourage their use. Finally, the attitudes, confidence, and self-esteem of preservice teachers seem to benefit from participation in microteaching.

MacLeod published two reviews aggregating research on microteaching. With regard to the microteaching process itself, he concludes that: visual displays or demonstrations are preferable to written descriptions of the target skills; use of both examples and non-examples are essential to discriminate between what are appropriate and inappropriate behaviors; a modeling/discrimination treatment may be just as effective as providing participant practice/feedback; and self-viewing or self-confrontation following the teaching skill episode, although not supported explicitly by studies he reviewed, is reasonable. With regard to the overall outcome, he notes, "What has become clear from the accumulated research is that the preparation phase of microteaching, incorporating modeling and discrimination training, can be of critical importance to the acquisition of teaching skills and that the role of practice . . . may be less critical than it has been assumed to be" (MacLeod 1987*a*, p. 538).

Protocol materials. Cruickshank and Haefele (1987) synthesized research on protocol materials (audio, visual, or written records of some important classroom or school-related event or phenomenon accompanied by theoretical knowledge that makes the event understandable). In their synthesis the studies are organized into four categories. One set of studies examined the effects of use of protocols by K-12 teachers on the subsequent behavior of their pupil learners. Another set examined the effects of use of protocols on teacher behavior itself. A third set focused on the effectiveness of protocols on concept acquisition. The fourth set investigated user reactions to the technical qualities and relevance of protocol materials. Among the generalizations from the studies are that: persons trained in the use of protocol materials find the experience enjoyable, they acquire the target concepts, they are able to demonstrate only some of them when teaching, and they benefit most from training that includes both concept acquisition and practice.

Reflective Teaching. This instructional approach refers to efforts that encourage preservice and inservice teachers to become more thoughtful and wise practitioners (Cruickshank 1987, Zeichner 1987). The original Reflective Teaching instructional model was developed at Ohio State University with support from philanthropic foundations. Research on Reflective Teaching has been generated by Beeler et al. (1985); Cruickshank, Kennedy, Williams, Holton, and Fay (1981); McKee (1986); Peters (1980); Peters and Moore (1980); and Troyer (1988).

Beeler and his colleagues focused mainly on improving the process of Reflective Teaching and found support for learner groups of 5 to 8 persons, rotating the membership in learner groups from lesson to lesson, choosing an especially interesting initial Reflective Teaching lesson, and selecting as the first designated teachers persons who will be enthusiastic about undertaking the teaching task.

Cruickshank and his colleagues compared pre-student teachers who had participated in Reflective Teaching sessions with those who had not and found that they differed in two ways. They were able to produce proportionally more analytic statements about teaching and learning, and they were "less anxious," "less frightened," and "more confident" about commencing student teaching.

McKee also studied the Reflective Teaching process and recommends videotaping the lessons so that the variety of teaching methods used by the various designated teachers can be reviewed and providing a summary of the main discoveries about teaching and learning posited by participants. Additionally, McKee reports that there is a high level of satisfaction among preservice teachers working with the Reflective Teaching model, and that it is an effective process for developing and refining skills in lesson preparation, delivery, and evaluation.

Peters compared Reflective Teaching with microteaching treatments (although they differ in purpose and means) and reports that subjects did not differ on the following criterion variables: attitudes toward teaching and the role of teachers or attitudes toward Reflective Teaching and microteaching. One Reflective Teaching group evidenced a higher self-perception of themselves as teachers. Peters and Moore in a similar study found essentially the same things, namely, no difference on the criterion variables studied.

Troyer investigated the effect of Reflective Teaching and a modification of it (the addition of a conceptual component) on the subjects' level of cognitive thought about teaching and learning. Her results strongly support that both Reflective Teaching and its modification have substantial effects on preservice teachers' level of reflection when analyzing classroom teaching. The treatments also had a significant effect on raising the explanatory/hypothetical, justificatory, and critical abilities of the subjects.

Simulation. Research on the use of simulation in teacher preparation programs was last summarized by Cruickshank (1971), although Copeland (1982) has addressed the topic briefly. Others who have studied this topic include Brand (1977); Cruickshank and Broadbent (1968); Emmer (1971); Gaffga (1967); Kauffman, Strang, and Loper (1985); Kersh (1963); Morine-Dershimer (1987); Twelker (1970); Vlcek (1966); and Wood, Combs, and Swan (1985).

Brand compared the effectiveness of two treatments (simulated encounters of classroom problems and traditional lecture/discussion of them) on pre-student teachers' attitudes toward pupils and teaching, on their responses to written hypothetical behavior problems, and on their later performance during student teaching when actually dealing with classroom problems. Following treatment, no difference in attitudes was found; but management behavior during student teaching favored the group receiving simulation training.

Cruickshank and Broadbent compared the effectiveness of a normal nine-week period of student teaching with a nine-week period consisting of two weeks of practice with simulated classroom problems plus seven weeks of regular student teaching. The primary dependent variable was the frequency of problems encountered by student teachers based on reports by their cooperating teachers. They found that the group provided exposure to and analysis of simulated problems prior to student teaching had fewer problems during student teaching.

Emmer investigated whether instructional behaviors learned and practiced while teaching college peers in a campus laboratory setting would transfer when early adolescents were brought in and became the learners. The results indicate that the target behaviors were learned while teaching peers and that their use was at least maintained when working with the early adolescents.

Gaffga used one of Cruickshank and Broadbent's field trials and found preservice teacher behavior during simulation to be a better predictor of subsequent student teaching performance than were similar predictions made by their former education professors.

Kauffman, Strang, and Loper developed a computer simulation in which preservice teachers teach a spelling lesson to four pupils portrayed on the screen. They found that the simulation meets specific criteria for realism and that the subjects teaching the spelling lesson respond in much the same way as they would if teaching actual children. Thus the simulation is successful in soliciting natural teaching behavior from users.

Kersh was interested in how authentic or realistic a simulation of classroom events must be. He compared the effectiveness of presentations of problematic classroom events in four formats: large "life-size" motion picture images, small motion picture images, large still-picture images, and small still-picture images. The object was to determine the number of practice trials required by pre-student teaching subjects to respond correctly to the simulation when presented in the different formats. This study provided mild support for use of simulations that portray problems using small still-picture images.

Morine-Dershimer's computer simulation was designed to train teachers in instructional decision making. Subjects were engaged in two computer-generated tasks, "Grouping for Instruction in Reading" and "Allotting Time for Instruction." The investigator reports that, in general, student reaction to the simulations is favorable. Also, the subjects are able to use computer-generated information to revise decisions about reading groups they have established.

Twelker made a major modification of Kersh's Classroom Simulator in order to make the regimen less labor intensive and thus less expensive to conduct. Two sets of simulation materials were developed, one presenting problems of classroom management, the other focusing on discovery teaching. Field tests reveal that the products are timely and credible but that their use did not cause all users to achieve proficiency.

Vlcek used a reproduction of Kersh's Classroom Simulator to assess its impact on preservice teacher users. Like Kersh, he found the simulator was

121

effective in shaping teacher responses to classroom problems. Furthermore, longer engagement with the simulator was related to subsequent, successful student teaching. The simulator experience seemed to be a factor in developing confidence in one's teaching ability.

Wood, Combs, and Swan assessed an interactive computer simulation that provides practice in planning and conducting a special education class in a hypothetical elementary school. It is intended for use by preservice and inservice teachers of severely emotionally or behaviorally handicapped pupils. Results include that the simulation is useful in meeting the target criteria (content validity, learning effectiveness, and efficiency).

Field experiences. Field experiences in teacher preparation programs are a much talked about but little studied phenomenon. However, according to Koehler (1985), there is an extensive body of research on supervising or cooperating teachers. Among her findings are that supervisory conferences are mostly sterile events, the cooperating teacher is the primary influence on the student teacher's instructional style, and university supervisors and cooperating teachers often share similar beliefs about teaching.

Early field experiences. Early field experiences (EFE), those taken prior to student teaching, have been the topic of studies by Applegate and Lasley (1983), Bates (1984), Denton (1982), Galluzzo and Arends (1989), Hedberg (1979), Ishler and Kay (1981), McIntyre and Killian (1986), Scherer (1979), and Sunal (1980), among others.

Applegate and Lasley surveyed 291 preservice teachers in eight Ohio colleges to determine their expectations of EFE. Subjects reported they want to learn the complexities of teaching, to see if they can model good professional practice, and to understand how education takes place in diverse, multicultural classrooms. Further, they intend to gather ideas about effective teaching and managing, to develop their own instructional style, and to work directly with pupils. Clearly, these subjects did not see distinctions between EFE and student teaching.

Bates investigated the attitudes of preservice teachers toward tutoring as an early field experience by having them tutor secondary pupils in reading in the content fields. Results revealed that overall the subjects' attitudes toward and expectations about tutoring were positive.

Denton investigated whether participation by secondary education majors in an EFE would affect their attainment of course objectives in a subsequent methods class. He found that the experimental group of 61 EFE preservice teachers outperformed the non-EFE control group on the criterion measures. They achieved greater cognitive gains and met a greater number of the course objectives.

122

Galluzzo and Arends note that data from the Research About Teacher Education Project reveal that special education preservice teachers average about 166 clock hours of EFE, followed by early childhood and elementary education majors with 140, and secondary majors with 90.

Hedberg investigated whether preservice teachers enrolled in an educational psychology course who participated in EFE (tutoring, small-group instruction, etc.) in lieu of part of their regular classroom instruction on campus would achieve as well on the final exam as those enrolled in a parallel course without field work. He found the EFE students peformed just as well, even though they had one-third less time of regular classroom instruction. In their survey of EFE practices, Ishler and Kay report that 99% of teacher preparation institutions offer EFE, and 80% of those require up to 150 contact hours in the field. The most commonly used EFE activities in order of frequency are: observation, tutoring, reporting on the classroom experience, performing non-instructional tasks, operating media, assessing pupil characteristics and activities, planning instruction, designing instructional materials, supervising extracurricular activities, assessing teacher characteristics, reviewing education literature, supervising laboratory work and field trips, and planning non-instructional activities. The least used EFE activites are: determining pupil grades, participating in parent conferences, attending professional meetings, teaching the whole class, and teaching small groups. Major problems associated with EFE include scheduling and transportation, not enough university personnel for supervision, and lack of cooperation by some local education agencies.

McIntyre and Killian compared EFE of elementary and secondary education majors. They report that elementary majors are more likely to be involved in EFE, to spend more contact hours in schools, to be gradually inducted into teaching, and to receive more feedback and correction regarding their work.

Scherer investigated whether preservice teachers who elected to participate in EFE differed from those who chose not to in terms of self-concept and classroom performance during student teaching. He found that EFE was associated with more positive self-concepts but not with better student teaching performance.

Sunal compared subjects in an elementary teacher education sequence consisting of methods courses supplemented with EFE with subjects in the same sequence of courses without EFE. Sunal found that the subjects with EFE demonstrated more and higher quality teacher behaviors at the end of the course sequence (before student teaching) when both groups were given the task of planning and teaching a three-lesson science unit to pupils in elementary classrooms.

123

Student Teaching. The literature on student teaching is vast and mostly polemic in nature. Several research reviews have captured the essence of the studies on this topic (Davies and Amershek 1969; Galluzzo and Arends 1989; Hersh, Hull, and Leighton 1982; Michaelis 1960; and Turney 1987).

Historically, the Michaelis review makes a good starting point. He makes clear that critical, evaluative research on student teaching is weak (p. 1473). Much of his research synthesis deals with demographic data about student teaching. For example, he reports that: the student teaching program typically has a university administrator; student teacher college supervisors usually are members of the education professoriate; assignments of student teachers are made cooperatively by university and local education agency personnel; the median student teacher college supervisory load was 13 in one study and 12 in another; and cooperating teachers receive a small honorarium or tuition remission. Among the critical problems identified are: obtaining qualified cooperating teachers and providing them with staff development, obtaining supervisory time for university personnel, compensating cooperating teachers adequately, and obtaining full school district cooperation. Admission to student teaching programs typically requires completion of prerequisite courses, a grade point average of C or better, and a health examination.

Studies to identify predictive criteria for preservice teachers' success in student teaching, which would be useful for admissions decisions, reveal some small promise for such personal factors such as high morale, confidence, social adaptability, and favorable attitudes toward children. Difficulties encountered by student teachers include classroom discipline, guidance of group activities, lesson preparation and presentation, routines, and relationships with superiors.

Davies and Amershek note an increase in student teaching-related research reported between the mid-Fifties and the mid-Sixties; but the actual number was small, with only 42 studies reported between 1964-66. Many of the studies, like those reviewed by Michaelis, provide demographic data. For example, few black or Caucasian education majors have opportunities to observe or student teach in integrated classrooms; most school districts provide student teaching opportunities; little uniformity exists in the procedures for administering student teaching programs; cooperating teachers prefer all-day, semester-long engagements; admission criteria for student teaching usually include grades in professional courses and physical, emotional, ethical, and moral fitness; universities finance the programs; and student teaching is required for certification in all states.

With regard to student teacher supervision the reviewers note: college supervisors (at that time) mostly were given one-half of a credit hour toward their workload for each student teacher supervised; cooperating teachers usually were required to be approved by the building principal; 40 states had no certification requirements for cooperating teachers; the typical load for cooperating teachers was two student teachers per year; and cooperating teachers' influence on student teachers is greater if their relationship with them has been formal.

With regard to student teachers, the reviewers found that student teaching can affect preservice teachers' attitudes depending on a number of factors: "Sharp positive change in the attitudes of student teachers toward children is associated with interaction with certain college supervisors, placement in lower grades, and a single rather than multiple student teaching placement" (p. 1382). Student teaching can affect preservice teachers' self-perceptions and perceptions of other teachers with regard to becoming more trusting and accepting and perceiving others as becoming so also.

Galluzzo and Arends report that the typical student teaching experience lasts 12 weeks and provides 12 hours of university credit, that the average ratio of college supervisors to student teachers is one to 18, and that college supervisors make an average of six visits to each student teacher.

Hersh, Hull, and Leighton offer a more extensive review of research and report on the dynamics of student teaching as well as provide demographic data. They report that most student teachers are placed in self-contained classrooms in small towns or suburbs but have few opportunities to work in kindergarten or middle/junior high schools. Student teachers typically are college seniors and spend 30 hours per week for 12 weeks in a school setting. Selection criteria for cooperating teachers include teaching competence, knowledge of subject matter, and willingness to serve. Cooperating teachers usually receive a small honorarium, but their primary reward is having the student teacher as a helper in the classroom. Student teachers often participate in weekly seminars conducted by the college supervisor; however, the impact of the seminars is unclear for the most part. There is a trend toward placing student teachers in centers or single schools, but no evidence exists that this centralization results in better student teacher performance.

Student teachers who have had early field experiences and simulation opportunities tend to perceive themselves as better prepared, as do their cooperating teachers and college supervisors. Student teaching in inner-city schools has a negative effect on self-image, is associated with custodial attitudes toward children, lowers self-confidence, reduces child-centeredness, and heightens a sense of self-protection. Student teachers in four-year baccalaureate programs usually are rated higher by their pupils than those from post-baccalaureate programs. Certain instructional experiences provided before or during student teaching that are reported to be beneficial include: self-analysis and awareness training, classroom observation, training in inquiry methods, non-verbal communication and enthusiasm, and use of simulation. Student teachers who received more indirect supervision and feedback seem to retain desired teaching behaviors over time. No relationship is apparent between supervisory style and success in student teaching. College supervisors, cooperating teachers, principals, and student teachers express substantial agreement on how student teachers should be evaluated. Poor management and discipline strategies are the most commonly cited reason for failure of student teachers.

Over time, student teachers' concerns change from anxiety about personal survival to concern about the results of their instruction and finally to the well-being of their pupils. They are anxious mostly about their relationships with pupils and supervisors but also are concerned about insufficient autonomy. The most notable shifts in student teachers' attitudes are away from idealism and open-mindedness and toward custodial and bureaucratic functions. Student teachers who are either extremely submissive or dominant are not likely to be judged successful teachers at a later time. Low levels of moral development are not associated with effective student teaching. Positive self-concept and being seen as venturesome are related to student teacher success. Student teachers are most effective when they share a common view of the teacher's role with their cooperating teacher. The cooperating teacher substantially influences the behavior of the student teacher mostly by modeling behaviors. Student teachers become more like their cooperating teachers in their behavior, attitudes, and expectations as time goes by.

Turney organizes his research review of student teaching under five headings: complexities and conflicts in supervision, supervisory influence, college supervisors, concerns of students, and clinical supervision. The clinical supervision section is mostly a description of the process and is not discussed here.

With regard to supervision, Turney notes that conflicts arise when one member of the student teaching triad (student teacher, cooperating teacher, and college supervisor) is excluded, when there are different perceptions regarding their roles, when there is a lack of opportunity to carry out their roles, when there are conflicts that inhibit carrying out their roles, and when there are personality differences, poor communication, and differing views with regard to effective practice.

With regard to supervisory influence and college supervisors, Turney, like Hersh et al., reports that cooperating teachers play a pivotal role in influencing student teachers. He cites a number of studies that found that, over the short term, the attitudes and instructional practices of student teachers become increasingly similar to their cooperating teacher models. Additionally, he notes that a supervisory style that emphasizes indirectness is related to high student teacher morale, that student teachers want analyses of their teaching performance but seldom receive it, that they need help from cooperating teachers mostly in the area of planning, and that they are concerned about the shortcomings of supervisory techniques. Supervisory techniques student teachers would like to see employed include taping lessons for later review and reflection and listing at the beginning of student teaching of what is expected of the student teacher.

With regard to the concerns of student teachers, Turney cites the research of Frances Fuller in which she identified three progressive phases of teacher concern: 1) concern about self, 2) concern about self as a teacher, and 3) concern about pupils. Additional concerns noted by Turney include: interpersonal relationships with the cooperating teacher and college supervisor; receiving clear and consistent expectations; and obtaining positive feedback, trust, support, understanding, and consideration.

Summary of Research on the Teacher Preparation Curriculum

Among the tentative findings related to the teacher preparation curriculum are the following. Regularly certified teachers are judged more effective. Student teachers in baccalaureate degree education programs are given higher marks by K-12 pupils than those in post-baccalaureate education programs. There is a positive relationship between teacher preparation coursework in science education and successful classroom performance. The curriculum is comprised mostly of general education, courses in the teaching content field, and courses in pedagogy including field experiences. The most frequently cited component of the curriculum required for state certification is student teaching, followed by courses in educational psychology, general methods (pedagogy), foundations, and teaching of reading.

Tentative findings for instruction include the following: Use of behavior modification in teacher preparation has promise; preservice teachers can learn to use it and when they do it works. There is support for the use of demonstration teaching with preservice teachers being able to later model the target behavior. Use of heuristics or inquiry approaches results in higher-level questioning in the classroom, particularly with less experienced teachers. Use of interaction analysis is associated with increased use of indirect teacher influence and more positive attitudes toward classroom observation. Mastery learning generally results in higher achievement. Use of microteaching results in increased acquisition of target teaching skills, and the acquisition process is enhanced when cooperating teachers use and reinforce student teacher use of the skills. Preservice teachers find protocol materials enjoyable, and they come to understand target concepts through their use. Reflective Teaching is valued by preservice teachers; it seems to promote higher-order thinking about teaching and learning and results in increased confidence in teaching. Simulation seems to result in desirable outcomes, including a reduction in the number of problems encountered during student teaching.

Preservice teachers are positively disposed toward field experiences. Early field experiences seem to be associated with cognitive gain in professional coursework and better pre-student teaching, but not necessarily better student teaching performance. Student teaching seems to be enhanced by such instructional practices as self-analysis and awareness, classroom observation, training in inquiry, non-verbal communication and enthusiasm, and use of simulation. Student teachers tend to become more like their cooperating teachers in behavior, attitudes, and expectations. When the student teaching assignment is in an inner-city school, the effect seems to be a more negative self-image, a more custodial attitude toward children, a diminution of child-centeredness, and a perceived need for self-protection.

The Education Professoriate

Troyer (1986) summarized research published since 1979 on what has been learned about teacher educators or the education professoriate. In addition to her work, other studies she did not identify or that have been published subsequently are summarized here (Blanchard 1982; Clark and Guba 1977; Condition of the Professoriate 1989; Darter 1980; Galluzzo and Arends 1989; Katz 1982; Myers and Mager 1985; Nussel, Wiersma, and Rusche 1988; Raths 1985; Research About Teacher Education Project 1987; Schuttenberg 1985; and Tamir and Peretz 1983).

Troyer's summary follows a taxonomy of professorial characteristics developed by Cruickshank (1984). It covers formative influences, present personal characteristics and abilities, present professional characteristics and abilities, and teaching behaviors and style.

Formative influences. Teacher educators are mostly from lower-middle and middle-class families with parents who are less well educated. For the most part, they are from rural areas and smaller cities. They tend to work in universities close to their home origin. As a group they hold a greater proportion of doctorates than their counterparts in other university departments.

Present personal characteristics and abilities. This category includes activity and energy level, physical and mental status, self-confidence, and social success. Most teacher educators report that they devote more than 40 hours a week to professional work and that teaching and advising occupy most of their time. Typically they teach three or four courses per academic period and spend four to nine contact hours each week in the classroom. They have heavy graduate advising responsibilities with much time devoted to doctoral candidates. One study found that education faculty as a whole have lower intelligence scores compared to those holding the doctorate in all fields. The same study reports that holders of the doctorate in education have lower mean high school class rankings and lower grade point averages in mathematics and science.

Present professional characteristics and abilities. This category covers ability to establish mutually satisfying relationships with professional colleagues, level of interest in teaching, knowledge of subject, and academic productivity. The majority of teacher education students report their education faculty to be experienced and able to offer clinical help, and they are very satisfied with coursework provided in education. One study notes the less experienced faculty at lower ranks tend to be less valued. Novice teacher educators engage in little interaction with their colleagues and participate little in professional organizations. Most teacher educators view teaching as their primary responsibility and prefer working with students to engaging in research or other professional activities. In one study, less than 1% of teacher educators polled indicated primary interest in scholarship; 75% reported that they had spent no time on scholarly activities in the week they were polled. Also, few reported they were involved in consulting or in pursuing grants or contracts.

One study reports only one-third of teacher educators had either authored or edited a book; fewer than half had written an article recently; and only 20% had written three or more articles in a designated three-year period. A parallel study reports 52% had an article accepted in the past year; 45% had published six or more articles during their career; 76% had published at least once. Another study found less than 20% of university teacher education units had faculty who were doing research or development work. Although teacher educators have a background of K-12 teaching experience providing them both contextual and clinical knowledge, some are assigned to teach in content areas in which they are not prepared either through academic coursework or staff development.

Teaching behaviors and style. Teacher educators report limited use of instructional alternatives, preferring instead to use whole class instruction (lecturing) and small-group work. Rarely do they use laboratory (practice-feedback) regimens such as microteaching, simulations, and protocols. Neither do they report research to preservice teachers or assign the reading of same.

Blanchard's study of the mental health status of teacher educators between 1976-1978 is based on questionnaire responses from 31,857 faculty representing 656 universities. Among other things, he reports that 30% have contemplated suicide; 50% are annoyed by their peers most of the time; 60% say students get on their nerves; 42% report tension and irritation are ongoing conditions; 38% worry a good part of the time; 42% experience mood swings, and about half have trouble sleeping.

Clark and Guba studied the education professoriate primarily to determine its scholarly productivity, but they also provide certain demographic data. Their sample included 8.6% of the then estimated 33,841 members of the education professoriate. (The sample intentionally over-represented institutions offering the doctorate.) They received responses from 1,387 faculty from 131 universities involved in teacher preparation. Data analyses revealed the following: The vast majority of education faculty hold the doctorate, ranging from 96% at private, research center, doctoral-level institutions to 62% at public institutions offering only preservice teacher education. The large majority of faculty received their doctorate at another university involved in teacher preparation. Doctoral-level institutions had the most experienced faculty. In general, most education faculty are associate professors and professors and therefore hold tenure. Turning to the scholarly productivity of the sample, the investigators note that "the evidence is overwhelming that knowledge production and utilization productivity . . . is concentrated in the doctoral-level institutions and particularly in . . . research center institutions" (p. V-29). They also point out that, overall, education faculty are dissatisfied with their current level of knowledge production and utilization.

The survey, *Conditions of the Professoriate*, revealed that education faculty differed from faculty in other fields as follows: Fewer thought that there had been a lowering of academic standards by universities, that students ill-suited to academic life are now enrolling, that students are seriously underprepared in basic skills, that undergraduates are willing to work hard, that students do only enough to get by, and that undergraduates are more willing to cheat. On the other hand, more thought undergraduates today are more academically competitive. In other matters, only 3% of education faculty said they were primarily interested in teaching. (Interestingly, 60% of faculty in mathematics and 53% in business/communications were primarily interested in teaching.) Education faculty were least likely to serve as paid consultants for business and industry, but 47% said they had been paid consultants in K-12 schools.

Darter examined the validity of the criticism that the K-12 school experience of education faculty is outdated and inadequate. A questionnaire designed to investigate education faculty qualifications was sent to 62 schools of education in public and private institutions in Texas. Results indicate that, for the most part, teacher educators have been removed from personal K-12 classroom teaching experience for some time. According to Darter, only 39% of his subjects had taught in lower schools within the previous 10 years. However, respondents reported they used a variety of activities to remain up-to-date, including supervision of field experiences, inservice work, and interactions with K-12 teachers and administrators.

Katz investigated the reputations of teacher education faculty among their students and among their university faculty peers. Results from her survey indicate that students rate the reputations of their teacher educators' more highly than do faculty peers in arts and sciences.

Myers and Mager investigated how education professors viewed their workplaces. Their sample included 537 education professors from 350 universities. Among their findings are that their respondents had insufficient time to do teaching, administer programs, do committee work, work with students, and engage in scholarship.

Nussel, Wiersma, and Rusche studied the work satisfaction of education professors. They obtained responses from 426 subjects representing 64 universities. Among their findings is that being a college professor is more satisfying for men, for tenured faculty, and for persons with rank of either professor or instructor. Overall, the investigators report a "rather high level of satisfaction, with certain administrative factors contributing to a decrease in satisfaction" (p. 50).

Raths queried 98 teacher educators from 32 institutions to determine their involvement in research. He reports only a small proportion carry out teacher education research, but they may be involved in research in their respective content fields.

The Research About Teacher Education Project (RATE) provides demographic information about education faculty and self-reports by faculty of secondary education methods regarding what they do and how they spend their time. Demographically, the total education faculty is 93% Caucasian, 70% Caucasian male, 75% tenured, has been employed in their present position an average of 13 years, and has an average of almost nine years experience in K-12 schools. Further, the report points out that the education professoriate increasingly will be populated by women, since women faculty are more likely to be younger, hold lower rank now but will advance in due course, and "dominate doctoral programs," which serve as the pool for new faculty. Regarding how secondary education faculty members spend their time, 60% is given to teaching, 22% to service, and 15% to scholarship. They report they spend 13 to 18 hours per month supervising six to nine student teachers, which is equated to teaching a three-credit course. The average number of courses taught per year is 7.5 at baccalaureate-level institutions, 8 at institutions where the master degree is the highest awarded, and 5 at doctoral-level institutions. Secondary education faculty report they would like to teach less and do more scholarship. With regard to scholarship, 25% of secondary teacher educators indicate that they have published 10 or more articles in refereed journals, while a like percentage has published none.

Galluzzo and Arends report further data about the education professoriate collected in the RATE Project. Notably, the professoriate is about two-thirds white male and one-quarter white female; males are in the majority at the rank of associate and professor. Average ages for assistant, associate, and professors respectively are 42, 47, and 53. About 90% of associates and assistants and two-thirds of assistants hold doctorates; more than 75% have tenure; and females are paid less at every rank.

Schuttenberg investigated the self-perceptions of 391 education faculty from 38 institutions regarding their scholarly productivity. Demographic data from the sample indicated the median age as 47; 65% are male; and 75% are tenured. Younger faculty perceived themselves to be more productive. The majority of the sample's perceptions regarding productivity had changed over the years with scholarship and service assuming increasing importance. Males were more accurate in their perception of actual scholarly productivity.

Tamir and Peretz also studied the reputation of teacher educators. This study, done in Israel and reported by Stewart (1986), reveals that the reputation of teacher educators was at least as good as that of other college instructors.

Summary of Research on the Education Professoriate

Members of the education professoriate might best be described as pedestrian in terms of their origins, abilities, academic prowess, and scholarly interests and productivity. They also could be characterized as hard-working and dedicated to their teaching and advising. Interestingly, although dedicated to teaching, they do not exhibit much variety in their use of instructional alternatives. They are perceived by preservice teachers as competent. Some researchers raises questions about their emotional well-being and about administrative factors that undermine work satisfaction.

The Context of Teacher Preparation

Of the principal variables constituting the field of teacher preparation, the one least studied is the context or environment where it takes place.

Clark and Guba (1977) conducted what is probably the most ambitious investigation of the context of teacher preparation. They found 72% or 1,367 of all U.S. institutions of higher education were in the business of teacher preparation. By contrast, according to Clifford and Guthrie (1988), in 1983 there were 202 university programs in business, 143 in engineering, 172 in law, and 74 in mass communications. Clark and Guba found that the state having the most was New York with 128; the state having the least was Wyoming with one. Institutions involved in teacher preparation fall into eight categories as follows:

1. Public doctoral level	112
2. Private doctoral level	51
3. Public master's level	248
4. Public master's level – regional campuses	36
5. Private master's level	278
6. Public baccalaureate level	66
7. Private baccalaureate level	550
8. Private baccalaureate level – regional campuses	26
Total	1367

A different categorization with greater specificity provides 12 options as follows:

1. Public research center institutions (doctoral level)	23
2. Private research center institutions (doctoral level)	11
3. Other public institutions with advanced graduate study (doctoral level)	89
4. Other private institutions with advanced graduate study (doctoral level)	40
5. Public pre/inservice teacher education centers (master's level)	183
6. Private pre/inservice teacher education centers (master's level)	75
7. Other public pre/inservice teacher education institutions	101

8. Other private pre/inservice teacher education institutions   203

9. Public preservice teacher education centers (baccalaureate level)   32

10. Private preservice teacher education centers (baccalaureate level)   104

11. Other public preservice teacher education institutions   60

12. Other private preservice teacher education institutions   <u>446</u>

Total   1367

Overall, 62% of the institutions were members of the American Association of Colleges for Teacher Education (AACTE). Membership in AACTE was best represented by the public institutions offering the doctorate (95%), compared to only 48% representation by the small, private baccalaureate level institutions. Regarding accreditation by the National Council for Accreditation of Teacher Education (NCATE), only 39% of all the teacher education institutions were accredited.

From a sample of 135 institutions, which was purposely non-representative in that it included 40 doctoral-level universities, it was found that the bulk of education graduates come from public institutions and that the largest producers of preservice teachers are institutions offering the highest degrees in education. However, the prototypical teacher preparing institution is a private, baccalaureate-level college with an enrollment of fewer than 1,000 students, graduating 67 to 70 preservice teachers each year, and having from one to five full-time equivalent faculty. Most of the education professoriate (69%) were found to work at public institutions that offer master's and doctoral degrees.

When deans of education in the study were asked to rate the emphasis given to knowledge production and utilization activities, they responded as follows: Deans of private research center, doctoral-level institutions saw the generation of both basic and applied research to be "central," while deans of counterpart public institutions saw the conduct of applied research and effecting change in schools as central. Deans of public doctoral-level education units ranked effecting change in schools, conducting inservice programs, and field service projects highest. Deans of public master's-level institutions also saw effecting school change and inservice work as central. No tendencies from baccalaureate institutions were noted.

On the matter of faculty load, 11 of the 12 research center, doctoral-level institutions reported that a minimum of 20% faculty time was allocated to knowledge production or utilization activities. Median teaching loads were eight hours per semester. Other doctoral-level education units also reported 20% to 25% of faculty time for scholary activities but larger teaching loads. Other types of institutions required a teaching load of 12 to 14 hours per semester.

Clark and Marker (1975) provide the following information about the teacher preparation workplace: Teacher preparation occurs in about 80% of approximately 1,400 four-year colleges and universities. Half of the universities preparing teachers graduate more than 175 to 200 teachers per year and the other half less than 175 to 200. However, the most typical program graduates 50 to 75. In all institutions, teacher preparation has both low prestige and low financial support. Only 40% of teacher preparation programs are NCATE accredited, but 85% have regional accreditation.

Peseau and Orr (1980) provide data from several studies showing that, for funding purposes, most states view teacher education as less complex and therefore less costly than other university programs. In one study, of the nine universities providing data, four teacher education programs were underfunded by 40% or more on the basis of return of tuition dollars generated by those programs. In fact, all nine were underfunded in the range of 12% to 62%. In another study of 46 teacher education programs in major state and land-grant universities, the investigators found that university officials do not share the beliefs of teacher educators regarding the role and needs of the teacher education program. They also report wide variations among the 29 institutions that provided complete data with regard to such things as class size (range from 2.89 to 25.34) and credit hours (range from 189 to 1,991) generated per faculty member. In these 29 institutions the cost of preservice teacher preparation was least in the programs with the highest enrollments. Notable is the finding that the average cost per student for an academic year in teacher education was $927. During that same year (1977-78), the national average per pupil expenditure in K-12 schools was $1,400; and in 1978-79, the average expenditure per full-time equivalent student in higher education was $2,363.

The Research About Teacher Education Project (1987) provides more recent data about the context of teacher preparation. Preservice teachers constitute 12% of undergraduates in baccalaureate-level teacher-preparing institutions. Institutions preparing teachers offer several routes to becoming a teacher: completion of a baccalaureate degree in education, completion of one of a variety of master's degree programs leading to certification, and completing a baccalaureate in an academic field and earning sufficient credits in education to meet state certification requirements. Ninety percent of the institutions surveyed offer teacher preparation in elementary education; 72% in physical education. At baccalaureate-level institutions, enrollments in the preservice teacher education are as follows: elementary education (35%), secondary education (18%), special education (12%), early childhood education (7%), and 28% in other specialties including K-12 physical education, reading, and home economics. Secondary education majors at the same institutions choose the following majors: mathematics (26%), English (25%), social sciences (24%), sciences (21%), and foreign languages (6%). Approximately three-fourths of the 76 AACTE institutions participating in the study had some or all of their programs nationally accredited.

Summary of Research on the Context of Teacher Preparation

Clearly, a large percentage of higher education institutions in this country are involved in teacher preparation. As many as 15% of them are not accredited by regional accrediting agencies and less than 40% are accredited by NCATE. Teacher preparation in many cases is poorly funded within the university. Data seem to indicate that less is spent to prepare a teacher than is spent to prepare the average university student or even a K-12 pupil.

Shortcomings of Research on Teacher Preparation

Evertson, Hawley, and Zlotnick (1985) address the limitations of research on teacher preparation. They note, "We acknowledge at the outset that although the number of studies related to teacher education is large, the research often is of dubious scientific merit and frequently fails to address the type of issues about which policymakers are most concerned" (p. 2). Koehler (1985) also sees a number of problems related to research on teacher education. She terms most of it "bootstrap research." "Most of these studies [those identified in an ERIC search], if funded at all, were small university grants − possibly support for a graduate student, some computer funds, and clerical help. Others were dissertations" (p. 25). Like Clark and Guba, Koehler contends the research is done on top of an already comparatively heavy teaching and advising load. She also faults the research for such technical problems as nature and size of samples, lack of reliability and validity checks, and faulty assumptions. Finally, she describes it as "particularistic" and corner-cutting (p. 28).

How Inquiry on Teacher Education Can Inform

Research on preservice teachers. Knowledge gained from the study of preservice teachers has many uses. First, in a descriptive sense, we can

136

learn a lot about them – their backgrounds and formative influences, their personal characteristics, why they choose to teach, and how long they intend to commit to teaching. Such information provides a profile that might be used in recruiting and retaining the future teacher force. It can be used to forecast teacher supply, to estimate the balance of males to females and of minorities to majority. Finally, it can be used to ascertain the quality of teacher candidates with respect to their abilities, attitudes, values, perceptions, and preferences. Such information can serve to guide futher research on who is most likely to be effective in the classroom. Using one of the research models described in Chapter One (Dunkin-Biddle or McDonald-Elias), it should be possible to predict which preservice teacher characteristics are associated with effective classroom behavior, thus giving us a better basis for enlightened admission into the teacher education program.

Research on the education professoriate. The few studies available in this area suggest that teacher educators are more oriented toward teaching and advising than toward scholarly endeavors. Further, conditions of the workplace, such as heavy teaching and advising loads, tend to deter the education professoriate from pursuing research that would provide a better knowledge base for their field. We also know that teacher educators as a group are relatively conservative in their instructional approaches, relying primarily on large-group lecture and discussion and neglecting some of the promising instructional alternatives. Of concern to the field in general are the findings of one study that suggest that the mental health of the education professoriate is precarious.

Research on the context of teacher preparation. Other than demographic data, little information is available on this topic. What we do know is that teacher education is big business in higher education institutions in this country. It also is one of the least expensive programs to administer, which may account for its presence on so many campuses. Unfortunately, we do not know whether big business equates with good business. We do know, however, that many teacher education institutions are not regionally accredited (about 15%) and that less than half have national accreditation. We assume, but do not know, that accreditation equates with effectiveness. That assumption might well be on the research agenda of the future.

Research on curriculum and instruction. Despite the lack of research, assertions about the weaknesses of the teacher preparation curriculum are commonplace. What research does tell us is that those who have completed a regular preservice program are more likely to be judged effective upon entering teaching, that coursework in education is positively associated with successful teaching (at least in science), that teachers can acquire the recently developed knowledge base on teaching (see Chapters Two, Three, and Four), and that preservice teachers generally have positive attitudes toward their professional preparation and consider it to be relatively rigorous.

On the other hand, the propensity of researchers to collect endless amounts of demographic data about the teacher preparation curriculum has not been particularly useful. To know only about the broad areas of the teacher preparation curriculum or the percentage of time given to these curriculum areas is of no particular significance. Given the models (see Chapter One) now available for guiding research on teacher education, we should be seeing more significant studies on the teacher preparation curriculum. Clearly, an enormous amount of inquiry needs to be done.

Research on instruction in teacher preparation is more promising. Research done to date on an array of instructional alternatives provides a measure of confidence for their use with preservice teachers. These include behavior modification, demonstration teaching, heuristics or inquiry learning, interaction analysis, mastery learning, microteaching, Reflective Teaching, simulation, and field experiences.

With regard to student teaching, research has shown that the cooperating teacher has a major influence on the professional behaviors of student teachers. Therefore, great care must be given to the selection of cooperating teachers who can serve as positive models. Also, because of adverse conditions in many inner-city classrooms, care must be exercised in placing student teachers there unless they can be placed with cooperating teachers with demonstrated effectivness in urban teaching.

What Else Do We Need to Know?

Much remains unknown about teaching and teacher education. We know very little about teacher educators as a group, particularly the qualities that enable them to help preservice students become effective teachers through their professional courses and later in the field. Simply put, we do not know what constitutes an effective teacher educator. Neither do we know very much about the specific nature of the teacher preparation curriculum, that is, what precisely is communicated to and learned by preservice teachers. We certainly do not know much about the relationship between what *actually* is taught and learned and later success in K-12 classrooms. In other words, the specific curriculum first needs to be determined and then validated.

Although we have some knowledge of instructional alternatives in teacher education, it remains to be determined which alternatives are most effective for the various curriculum components. Also, we do not know the optimal conditions, both physical and psychological, for the context of the teacher preparation program. Most importantly, we need to know what personal attributes should be considered for admitting students to the preservice program. What characteristics, beyond completing the required courses, predict success as a K-12 teacher?

Finally, we need to know how the five principal variables in teacher preparation (teacher educators, preservice teachers, contexts where teacher preparation occurs, curriculum content, and instruction) interact and influence each other. And we need to know how and how much the variables, individually and collectively, contribute to the preparation of effective teachers, however defined.

References

Allen, C.T., and Forman, S.G. "Efficacy of Methods of Training Teachers in Behavior Modification." *School Psychology Review* 13 (1984): 26-32.

Andrew, M.D. "The Characteristics of Students in a Five-Year Teacher Education Program." *Journal of Teacher Education* 34, no. 1 (1983): 20-23.

Andrews, J.K. "The Results of a Pilot Program to Train Teachers in the Classroom Application of Behavior Modification Techniques." *Journal of School Psychology* 8 (1970): 37-42.

Applegate, J., and Lasley, T. "What Undergraduates Expect from Preservice Field Experience." Paper presented at the annual meeting of the American Educational Research Association, Montreal, 1983.

Bates, G. "The Effects of Early Field Experience Tutoring in Reading on Secondary Majors' Attitudes, Expectations, and Effectiveness." Paper presented at the annual meeting of the American Educational Research Association, New Orleans, 1984.

Beeler, K.; Kayser, G.; Matzner, K.; and Saltmarsh, R. "Reflective Teaching: Reflections on College Classroom Experiences." *Educational Journal* 18 (Fall 1985): 4-9.

Blanchard, B. "The Mental Health of College and University Professors Engaged in Teacher Education." *Scientia Paedagogica Experimentalis* 19 (1982): 249-68. ERIC No. 228 959

Bondi, J.C. "Feedback from Interaction Analysis: Some Implications for the Improvement of Teaching." *Journal of Teacher Education* 21 (1970): 189-96.

Bontempo, B., and Digman, S. "Entry Level Profile: Student Attitudes Toward the Teaching Profession." Paper presented at the annual meeting of the American Educational Research Association, Chicago, 1985. ERIC No. 258 949

Book, C.; Byers, J.; and Freeman, D. "Student Expectations and Teacher Education Traditions with Which We Can and Cannot Live." *Journal of Teacher Education* 34 (January/February 1983): 9-13.

Book, C., and Freeman, D. "Differences in Entry Characteristics of Elementary and Secondary Teacher Candidates." *Journal of Teacher Education* 37, no. 2 (1986): 47-51.

Book, C.; Freeman, D.; and Brousseau, B. "Comparing Academic Backgrounds and Career Aspirations of Education and Non-Education Majors." *Journal of Teacher Education,* 36, no. 3 (1985): 27-30.

Borko, H.; Lalik, R.; and Tomchin, E. "Student Teachers' Understandings of Successful and Unsuccessful Teaching." *Teaching and Teacher Education* 3, no. 2 (1987): 77-90.

Bowles, P.E., and Nelson, R.O. "Training Teachers as Mediators: Efficacy of a Workshop Versus the Bug-in-the-Ear Technique." *Journal of School Psychology* 14 (1976): 15-26.

Brand, M. "Effectiveness of Simulation Techniques in Teaching Behavior Management." *Journal of Research in Music Education* 25 (1977): 131-38.

Brown, J.C.; Montgomery, R.; and Barclay, J.R. "An Example of Psychologist Management of Teacher Reinforcement Procedures in the Elementary Classroom." *Psychology in the Schools* 6 (1969): 336-40.

Callahan, R. "A Study of Teacher Candidates' Attitudes." *College Students Journal* 14, no. 2 (1980): 167-75.

Carnegie Foundation for the Advancement of Teaching. "Future Teachers: Will There Be Enough Good Ones?" *Change* 18, no. 5 (1986): 27-30.

Clark, C.; Guskey, T.; and Bennings, J. "The Effectiveness of Mastery Learning Strategies in Undergraduate Education Courses." *Journal of Educational Research* 76, no. 4 (1983): 210-14.

Clark, D., and Guba, E. *A Study of Teacher Education Institutions as Innovators, Knowledge Producers, and Change Agencies, Final Report.* National Institute of Education Project No. 4-0752. Bloomington, Ind.: Indiana University, 1977. Note: A summary appears as Guba, E., and Clark D. "Knowledge Production and Use in Schools, Colleges and Departments of Education." *Phi Delta Kappan* (May 1977): 711-13.

Clark, D., and Marker, G. "The Institutionalization of Teacher Education." In *Teacher Education, Seventy-Fourth Yearbook of the National Society for the Study of Education,* edited by K. Ryan. Chicago: University of Chicago Press, 1975.

Clifford, G., and Guthrie, J. *Ed School: A Brief for Professional Education.* Chicago: University of Chicago Press, 1988.

Condition of the Professoriate: Attitudes and Trends, 1989. Lawrenceville, N.J.: Princeton University Press, 1989.

Cooper, M.L.; Thomson, C.L.; and Baer, D.M. "The Experimental Modification of Teacher Attending Behavior." *Journal of Applied Behavior Analysis* 3 (1970): 153-57.

Cooperman, S., and Klagholz, L. "New Jersey's Alternate Route to Teacher Certification." *Phi Delta Kappan* 66 (June 1985): 691-95.

Copeland, W. "Laboratory Experiences in Teacher Education." In *Encyclopedia of Educational Research,* Fifth Ed., edited by H. Mitzel. New York: Free Press, 1982.

Cossairt, A.; Hall, R.V.; and Hopkins, B.L. "The Effects of Experimenter's Instructions, Feedback, and Praise on Teacher Praise and Student Attending Behavior." *Journal of Applied Behavior Analysis* 6 (1973): 89-100.

Cotten, D.R.; Evans, J.J.; and Tseng, M.S. "Relating Skill Acquisition to Science Classroom Teaching Behavior." *Journal of Research in Science Teaching* 15 (1978): 187-95.

Cruickshank, D. *Reflective Teaching: The Preparation of Students of Teaching.* Reston, Va.: Association of Teacher Educators, 1987.

Cruickshank, D. *Models for the Preparation of America's Teachers.* Bloomington, Ind.: Phi Delta Kappa Educational Foundation, 1985.

Cruickshank, D. "Toward a Model to Guide Inquiry in Preservice Teacher Education." *Journal of Teacher Education* 35, no. 6 (1984): 43-48.

Cruickshank, D. "Teacher Education Looks at Simulation." In *Educational Aspects of Simulation,* edited by P. Tansey. London: McGraw-Hill, 1971.

Cruickshank, D., and Broadbent, F. *The Simulation and Analysis of Problems of Beginning Teachers.* Research Project No. 5-0789. Washington, D.C.: U.S. Government Printing Office, 1968. ERIC No. 024 637.

Cruickshank, D., and Haefele, D. "Teacher Preparation Via Protocol Materials." *International Journal of Educational Research* 11, no. 5 (1987): 543-55.

Cruickshank, D.R.; Kennedy, J.; Williams, J.; Holton, J.; and Fay, D. "Evaluation of Reflective Teaching Outcomes." *Journal of Educational Research* 75, no. 1 (1981): 26-32.

Darter, C., Jr. "Qualifications of Professional Education Faculty." Washington, D.C.: ERIC Clearinghouse on Teacher Education, 1980. ERIC No. 257 807

Davies, D., and Amershek, K. "Student Teaching." In *Encyclopedia of Educational Research,* Fourth Ed., edited by R. Ebel. New York: Macmillan, 1969.

Denton, J. "Early Field Experience Influence on Performance in Subsequent Coursework." *Journal of Teacher Education* 33, no. 2 (1982): 19-23.

Domas, S., and Tiedeman, D. "Teacher Competence: An Annotated Bibliography." *Journal of Experimental Education* 19 (1950): 99-218.

Dravland, V., and Greene, M. "A Comparison of Students Who Enter Education with Those Who Do Not." Paper presented at the annual meeting of the Canadian Society for the Study of Education, Montreal, 1980. ERIC No. 191 826

Druva, C., and Anderson, R. "Science Teacher Characteristics by Teacher Behavior and by Student Outcome: A Meta-Analysis of Research." *Journal of Research in Science Teaching* 20, no. 5 (1983): 467-79.

Dumas, W., and Weible, T. "Standards for Elementary School Certification: A Fifty-State Study." *Elementary School Journal* 85, no. 2 (1984): 177-83.

Dupois, M. "Good Sign for Education Majors." *Education.* College of Education Alumni Newsletter, Pennsylvania State University, 8 (Spring 1984): 4.

Emmer, E.T. "Transfer of Instructional Behavior and Performance Acquired in Simulated Teaching." *Journal of Educational Research* 65, no. 4 (1971): 178-82.

Evertson, C.; Hawley, W.; and Zlotnick. "Making a Difference in Educational Quality Through Teacher Education." *Journal of Teacher Education* 36, no. 3 (1985): 2-12.

Fisher, R., and Feldman, M. "Some Answers About the Quality of Teacher Education Students." *Journal of Teacher Education* 36, no. 3 (1985): 37-40.

Flanders, N.A. *Helping Teachers Change Their Behavior.* Project Numbers 1721012 and 7-32-0560-171.0. Washington, D.C.: U.S. Office of Education, 1963.

Frank, B. "Cognitive Styles and Teacher Education: Field Dependence and Areas of Specialization Among Teacher Education Majors." *Journal of Educational Research* 80 (September-October 1986): 19-22.

Furst, N. "The Effects of Training in Interaction Analysis on the Behavior of Student Teachers in Secondary Schools." In *Interaction Analysis: Theory, Research and Application*, edited by E.J. Amidon and J.B. Hough. Reading, Mass.: Addison-Wesley, 1967.

Gaffga, R. "Simulation: A Model for Observing Student Teacher Behavior." Doctoral dissertation, University of Tennessee, 1967.

Gallegos, A., and Gibson, H. "Are We Sure the Quality of Teacher Candidates Is Declining?" *Phi Delta Kappan* 64 (September 1982): 33.

Galluzzo, G., and Arends, R. "The RATE Project: A Profile of Teacher Education Institutions." *Journal of Teacher Education* 40 (July-August 1989): 56-58.

George, K.D., and Nelson, M.A. "Effect of an Inservice Science Workshop on the Ability of Teachers to Use the Techniques of Inquiry." *Science Education* 55 (1971): 163-69.

Guyton, E., and Forokhi, E. "Academic Comparisons of Teacher Education Students and Non-Teacher Education Students." *Capstone Journal of Education* 6, no. 1 (1985): 21-31.

Hedberg, J. "The Effects of Field Experience on Achievement in Educational Psychology." *Journal of Teacher Education* 30, no. 1 (1979): 75-76.

Henjum, A. "A Study of the Significance of Student Teachers' Personality Characteristics." *Journal of Teacher Education* 20, no. 2 (1969): 143-47.

Hersh, R.; Hull, R.; and Leighton, M. "Student Teaching." In *Encyclopedia of Educational Research*, Fifth Ed., edited by H. Mitzel. New York: Free Press, 1982.

Horton, G.O. "Generalization of Teacher Behavior as a Function of Subject Matter Specific Discrimination Training." *Journal of Applied Behavior Analysis* 8 (1975): 311-19.

Horton, J.; Daniel, B.; and Summers, J. "A Decade of Change in Teacher Education: Results of a Ten-Year Study on Quality and Personal Characteristics of Teacher Candidates." *Contemporary Education* 56 (Summer 1985): 252-56.

Hough, J.B., and Amidon, E.J. "Behavioral Change in Student Teachers." In *Interaction Analysis: Theory, Research and Application*, edited by E.J. Amidon and J.B. Hough. Reading, Mass.: Addison-Wesley, 1967.

Hough, J.B.; Lohman, E.E.; and Ober, R. "Shaping and Predicting Verbal Teaching Behavior in a General Methods Course." *Journal of Teacher Education* 20 (1969): 213-24.

Hough, J.B., and Ober, R. "The Effect of Training in Interaction Analysis on the Verbal Teaching Behavior of Preservice Teachers." Paper presented at the annual meeting of the American Educational Research Association, Chicago, 1966. ERIC No. 011 252

Howey, L.; Yarger, S.; and Joyce, B. "Reflections on Preservice Preparation: Impressions from the National Survey." *Journal of Teacher Education* 29, no. 1 (1978): 38-40.

Hurst, J.B. "Competency-Based Modules and Inquiry Teaching." *Journal of Experimental Education* 43, no. 2 (1974): 35-39.

Ishler, R. "Requirements for Admission to and Graduation from Teacher Education." *Phi Delta Kappan* 66 (October 1984): 121-22.

Ishler, P., and Kay, R. "Exploratory Field Experiences: A Survey of Institutional Practices." In *Exploratory Field Experiences in Teacher Education*, edited by C. Webb, N. Gehrke, P. Ishler, and A. Mendoza. Reston, Va.: Association of Teacher Educators, 1981.

Jantzen, J.M. "Why College Students Choose to Teach: A Longitudinal Study." *Journal of Teacher Education* 23 (March-April 1982): 45-48.

Johnson, J.L., and Sloat, K.C.M. "Teacher Training Effects: Real or Illusory?" *Psychology in the Schools* 17 (1980): 109-15.

Joseph, P., and Green, N. "Perspectives on Reasons for Becoming Teachers." *Journal of Teacher Education* 37, no. 6 (1986): 28-33.

Joyce, B.; Yarger, S.; Howey, K.; Harbeck, K.; and Kluwin, T. *Preservice Teacher Education*. Contract No. PEC-O-74-9279. Palo Alto, Calif.: Center for Educational Research and Development, 1977. ERIC No. 146 120

Katz, L. "Reputations of Teacher Educators Among Members of Their Role Set." Paper presented at the annual meeting of the American Educational Research Association, New York, 1982. ERIC No. 213 486

Kauffman, J.; Strang, H.; and Loper, A. "Using Microcomputers to Train Teachers of the Handicapped." *Remedial and Special Education* 6, no. 5 (1985): 13-17.

Kemper, R., and Mangieri, J. "Student Interest in Teaching: Implications for Recruitment." *Teacher Educator* 20, no. 4 (1985): 19-24.

Kersh, B. *Classroom Simulation: A New Dimension in Teacher Education*. Final Report, Title VII, Project Number 886, National Defense Education Act of 1958, Grant No. 7-47-0000-164. Washington, D.C.: Department of Health, Education and Welfare, 1963.

Kirk, J. "Elementary School Student Teachers and Interaction Analysis." In *Interaction Analysis: Theory, Research and Application*, edited by E.J. Amidon and J.B. Hough. Reading, Mass.: Addison-Wesley, 1967.

Kluender, M. "Teacher Education Programs in the 1980s: Some Selected Characteristics." *Journal of Teacher Education* 35 (July-August 1984): 33-35.

Koehler, V. "Research on Preservice Teacher Education." *Journal of Teacher Education* 36, no. 1 (1985): 23-30.

Lange, D. "An Application of Social Learning Theory in Affecting Change in a Group of Student Teachers Using Video Modeling Techniques." *Journal of Educational Research* 65, no. 4 (1971): 151-54.

143

Langer, D., and Allen, G.E. *The Minicourse as a Tool for Training Teachers in Interaction Analysis.* Paper presented at the annual meeting of American Educational Research Association, Minneapolis, Minn., 1970. ERIC No. 037 393

Lanier, J., and Little, J. "Research on Teacher Education." In *Handbook of Research on Teaching,* Third Ed., edited by M. Wittrock. New York: Collier Macmillan, 1986.

Lohman, E.E.; Ober, R.; and Hough, J.B. "A Study of the Effect of Pre-Service Training in Interaction Analysis on the Verbal Behavior of Student Teachers." In *Interaction Analysis: Theory, Research and Application,* edited by E.J. Amidon and J.B. Hough. Reading, Mass.: Addison-Wesley, 1967.

Lombard, A.S.; Konicek, R.D.; and Schultz, K. "Description and Evaluation of an Inservice Model for Implementation of a Learning Cycle Approach in the Secondary Science Classrooms." *Science Education* 69 (1985): 491-500.

Luebkemann, H.H. "The Effects of Selected Student Teaching Program Variables on Certain Values and Certain Verbal Behaviors of Student Teachers." Doctoral dissertation, Pennsylvania State University, 1965.

MacLeod, G. "Microteaching: End of a Research Era?" *International Journal of Educational Research* 11, no. 5 (1987): 531-42. a

MacLeod, G. "Microteaching: Modeling." In *The International Encyclopedia of Teaching and Teacher Education,* edited by M.J. Dunkin. Elmsford, N.Y.: Pergamon, 1987. b

Matczynski, T.; Siler, E.R.; McLaughlin, M.L.; and Smith, J.W.R. "A Comparative Analysis of Achievement in Arts and Science Courses by Teacher Education and Non-Teacher Education Graduates." *Journal of Teacher Education* 39 (May-June 1988): 32-36.

McIntyre, D., and Killian, J.E. "Students' Interactions with Pupils and Cooperating Teachers in Early Field Experience." *Teacher Educator* 22, no. 2 (1986): 2-9.

McKee, A. *Reflective Teaching as a Strategy in TAFE Teacher Education.* Paper presented at the South Pacific Association of Teacher Education Conference, Perth, Australia, March 1986.

Medley, D. "Teacher Effectiveness." In *Encyclopedia of Educational Research,* Fifth Ed., edited by H. Mitzel. New York: Free Press, 1982.

Michaelis, J. "Teacher Education: Student Teaching and Internship." In *Encyclopedia of Educational Research,* edited by C. Harris. New York: Macmillan, 1960.

Morine-Dershimer, G. "Creating a Recycling Center for Teacher Thinking." In *Simulation and Clinical Knowledge in Teacher Education,* edited by E. Doak. Knoxville: University of Tennessee College of Education, 1987.

Myers, B., and Mager, G. *Professors' Observations on Their Work.* Paper presented at the annual meeting of the American Educational Research Association, Chicago, 1985. ERIC No. 257 813

Nelli, E. "A Research-Based Response to Allegations that Education Students Are Academically Inferior." *Action in Teacher Education* 6, no. 3 (1984): 73-80.

Nelson, F. "New Perspectives on the Teacher Quality Debate: Empirical Evidence from the National Longitudinal Survey." *Journal of Educational Research* 78, no. 3 (1985): 133-40.

Nussel, E.; Wiersma, W.; and Rusche, P. "Work Satisfaction of Education Professors." *Journal of Teacher Education* 39 (May-June 1988): 45-50.

Nutter, N. "Why Students Drop Out of Teacher Education." *Action in Teacher Education* 5 (1983): 25-32.

Olsen, D. "The Quality of Prospective Teachers: Education vs. Non-Education
Graduates." *Journal of Teacher Education* 36, no. 5 (1985): 56-59.

Peseau, B., and Orr, P. "The Outrageous Underfunding of Teacher Education."
Phi Delta Kappan 62 (October 1980): 100-102.

Peck, R., and Tucker, J. "Research on Teacher Education." In *Handbook of Research on Teaching*, Second Ed., edited by R. Travers. Chicago: Rand McNally, 1973.

Peters, J. "Effects of Laboratory Teaching Experience, Microteaching and Reflective Teaching in an Introductory Teacher Education Course on Students' Views
of Themselves as Teachers and Their Perceptions of Teaching." Doctoral dissertation, Ohio State University, 1980.

Peters, J., and Moore, G. *A Comparison of Two Methods of Providing Laboratory
Experiences for Student Teachers in Agriculture Education*. West Lafayette, Ind.:
Purdue University, 1980. ERIC No. 210 468

Phillips, D. "A Study of the Demographic, Developmental and Learning Style
Characteristics of Preservice Education Students." Doctoral dissertation, Ohio
State University, 1982.

Pigge, F. "Teacher Education Graduates: Comparisons of Those Who Teach and
Those Who Do Not Teach." *Journal of Teacher Education* 36, no. 4 (1985):
27-28.

Pigge, F., and Marso, R. "Relationships Between Student Characteristics and
Changes in Attitudes, Concerns, Anxieties, and Confidence About Teaching During Teacher Preparation." *Journal of Educational Research* 81, no. 2 (1987):
109-15.

Porterfield, D. "Infuence of Inquiry-Discovery Science Preparation on Questioning Behavior of Reading Teachers." *Reading Teacher* 27 (1974): 589-93.

Putnam, J. "Perceived Benefits and Limitations of Teacher Educator Demonstration Lessons." *Journal of Teacher Education* 36, no. 4 (1985): 36-41.

Putnam, R. "Structuring and Adjusting Content for Students: A Study of Live and
Simulated Tutoring of Addition." *American Educational Research Journal* 24
(Spring 1987): 13-48.

Raths, J. "Scholarly Activities of Teacher Educators." Paper presented at the annual meeting of the American Educational Research Association, Chicago, 1985.
ERIC No. 257 793

Research About Teacher Education Project. *Teaching Teachers: Facts and Figures*.
Washington, D.C.: American Association of Colleges for Teacher Education, 1987.

Riccobono, J.; Henderson, L.; Burkheimer, G.; Place, C.; and Levinjohn, J. *Na-
tional Longitudinal Study: Base Year (1972) Through Fourth Follow-up (1979)
Data File User's Manual*. Research Triangle Park, N.C.: Center for Education
Research, 1981.

Richardson, D., and Briggs, D.L. "Personal Characteristics of Secondary Student Teachers." *Clearing House* 57, no. 1 (1983): 28-29.

Ringer, U. "The Use of a 'Token Helper' in the Management of Classroom Behavior Problems and in Teacher Training." *Journal of Applied Behavior Analysis* 6 (1973): 671-77.

Roberson, D.; Keith, T.; and Page, E. "Now Who Aspires to Teach?" *Educational Researcher* 12 (June/July 1983): 13-21.

Robin, A. "Behavioral Instruction in the College Classroom." *Review of Educational Research* 46 (1976): 313-54.

Savage, T.V. "The Academic Qualifications of Women Choosing Education as a Major." *Journal of Teacher Education* 34, no. 1 (1983): 14-19.

Sandefur, J.T.; Pankratz, R.; and Couch, J. *Observation and Demonstration in Teacher Education by Closed-Circuit Television and Video-Tape Recordings.* Final Report, Research Project No. 5-1009, Title VII-A, NPEA, PL. 85-864. Emporia: Kansas State Teachers College, 1967. ERIC No. 014 904

Scherer, C. "Effects of Early Field Experience on Student Teachers' Self-Concepts and Performance." *Journal of Experimental Education* 47 (1979): 208-14.

Schuttenberg, E. "Self-Perceptions of Productivity of Education Faculty: Life Phase and Gender Differences." Paper presented at the annual meeting of the American Educational Research Association, Chicago, 1985. ERIC No. 257 807

Sharp, L., and Hirshfeld, S. *Who Are the New Teachers? A Look at 1971 College Graduates.* Washington, D.C.: Bureau of Social Science Research, 1975. ERIC No. 115 582

Skipper, C., and Quantz, R. "Changes in Educational Attitudes of Education and Arts and Sciences Students During Four Years of College." *Journal of Teacher Education* 38, no. 3 (1987): 39-44.

Sloat, K.C.M.; Tharp, R.G.; and Gallimore, R. "The Incremental Effectiveness of Classroom-Based Teacher Training Techniques." *Behavior Therapy* 8 (1977): 810-18.

Stewart, D. "Materials on the Education Professoriate in the ERIC Data Base." *Journal of Teacher Education* 37 (September-October 1986): 24-26.

Stolee, M. "Studies on Education Students at the University of Wisconsin-Milwaukee." *AACTE Briefs* 3, no. 6 (1982): 9.

Sunal, D. "Effect of Field Experience During Elementary Methods Courses on Preservice Teacher Behavior." *Journal of Research in Science Teaching* 17, no. 1 (1980): 17-23.

Tamir, P., and Peretz, M. "The Professional Image and Reputation of Teacher Educators in Israel." Paper presented at the annual meeting of the American Educational Research Association, Montreal, 1983. ERIC No. 228 214

Teacher Education Reports. Washington, D.C.: Feistritzer Publications, 22 September 1988.

Thomson, C.L., and Cooper, M.L. *The Modification of Teacher Behaviors Which Modify Child Behaviors.* Technical Research Report No. 19. Lawrence, Kan.: Head Start Evaluation and Research Center, 1969. ERIC No. 042 499

Troyer, M. "The Effects of Reflective Teaching and a Supplemental Theoretical Component on Preservice Teachers' Reflectivity in Analyzing Classroom Teaching Situations." Doctoral dissertation, Ohio State University, 1988.

Troyer, M. "A Synthesis of Research on the Characteristics of Teacher Educators." *Journal of Teacher Education* 37 (September-October 1986): 6-10.

Turney, C. "Supervision of the Practicum." In *International Encyclopedia of Teaching and Teacher Education*, edited by M. Dunkin. Oxford, England: Pergamon Press, 1987.

Turney, C.; Clift, J.; Dunkin, M.; and Traill, R. *Microteaching: Research, Theory and Practice*. Sydney, Australia: Sydney University Press, 1973.

Twelker, P. *Development of Low-Cost Simulation Materials for Teacher Education*. U.S. Office of Education Cooperative Research Project No. 5-0916. Monmouth, Ore.: State System of Higher Education, Teaching Research, 1970.

Vance, V.S., and Schlechty, P.C. "The Distribution of Academic Ability in the Teaching Force: Policy Implications." *Phi Delta Kappan* 64 (September 1982): 22-27.

Vlcek, C. "Assessing the Effect and Transfer Value of a Classroom Simulator Technique." Doctoral dissertation, Michigan State University, 1966.

Weaver, W.T. "In Search of Quality: The Need for Talent in Teaching." *Phi Delta Kappan* 61 (September 1979): 29-46.

Weible, T., and Dumas, W. "Secondary Teacher Certification Standards in Fifty States." *Journal of Teacher Education* 33, no. 4 (1982): 22-23.

Wood, K. "What Motivates Students to Teach?" *Journal of Teacher Education* 29, no. 6 (1978): 48-50.

Wood, M.; Combs, C.; and Swan, W. "Computer Simulations: Field Testing Effectiveness and Efficacy for Inservice and Preservice Teacher Preparation." *Journal of Educational Technology Systems* 14, no. 1 (1985): 61-74.

Woolfolk, A.E., and Woolfolk, R.L. "A Contingency Management Technique for Increasing Student Attention in a Small Group Setting." *Journal of School Psychology* 12 (1974): 204-12.

Yarger, S.; Howey, K.; and Joyce, B. "Reflections on Preservice Preparation: Impressions from the National Survey." *Journal of Teacher Education* 28, no. 6 (1977): 34-37.

Zeichner, K. "Preparing Reflective Teachers: An Overview of Instructional Strategies Which Have Been Employed in Preservice Teacher Education." *International Journal of Educational Research* 11, no. 5 (1987): 565-75.

Zevin, J. "Training Teachers in Inquiry." *Social Education* 37 (1973): 310-16.

6 Review and Recommendations

In this work I have attempted to contribute to the generation and use of knowledge that informs K-12 teaching and teacher preparation. One way to generate this knowledge is to employ inquiry models that take account of the principal components or variables operating in the systems known as teaching and teacher education. Once the components of each system are known and understood, each can be studied, as can their interactions.

In Chapter One, three inquiry models for study of the system of teaching were presented: Dunkin and Biddle (Figure 1), McDonald and Elias (Figure 2), and Medley (Figure 3). These three models have many commonalities. All include the principal actors (pupils and teachers), events, and contexts; the interactions among them; and the places where the interactions take place. Beyond that, the models suggest other variables affecting each of the principal ones. For example, Dunkin and Biddle suggest that pupils' present behaviors are functions of heredity and environmental factors. McDonald and Elias see teachers' classroom performances as functions of a great many factors, including their attitudes, aptitudes, expectations, and knowledge of subject matter and teaching methods. Medley sees learning as being affected by individual pupil characteristics and by the kinds of experiences provided. Another common feature of the models is the recognition that teacher education is an important factor influencing what teachers are like and what they do. Thus teaching and teacher education are intertwined and, to a point, inseparable. Tables 1 and 2, which organize and expand on the principal variables, should be of particular interest to persons disposed toward knowledge production.

Additionally in Chapter One, several models of the system of teacher preparation are described. They, too, share many commonalities as to the principal components or variables that are operating in the system of teacher preparation. The Cruickshank model (Figure 4), posits significant interactions among the components or variables. To encourage knowledge use, selected research that can serve to inform teaching and teacher preparation is presented in Chapters Two, Three, Four, and Five. This research can help to answer the questions: What is known about effective schooling? What is known about educational practice? What is known about teaching? What is known about teacher preparation? For teachers, the research is a source of data that can guide instructional decisions and behavior. For teacher educators, it is a source that can inform the selection of candidates for the preservice program and the substance of the professional curriculum.

From the research on effective schools reported in Chapter Two, a number of investigators have found certain school processes to be promising. These processes deserve special consideration. As other variables are studied more fully, they also may come to be considered promising.

Chapter Three summarizes research on what is known about effective K-12 educational practices. It reports a number of instructional practices that seem to hold promise for greater pupil learning and lists home and school practices considered to be effective based on reseach and opinion compiled by the U.S. Department of Education.

Research reported in Chapter Four identifies many behaviors associated with effective teaching. Several studies lend support to the effectiveness of certain teacher behaviors. Although not all behaviors were examined in all studies, even behaviors with support from a single study cannot be dismissed. Research on teacher education reported in Chapter Five is relevant primarily to teacher educators, although K-12 teachers should find it interesting since they have been through teacher education programs and many of them have served, or will serve, as cooperating teachers. Research on reasons for choosing teaching as a career, on comparisons of education and non-education majors, and on state certification requirements are continuing concerns for the profession as a whole.

Recommendations

Compiling, reviewing, and presenting the research reported in this volume has led me to suggest some actions, which I will make in the form of eight recommendations.

1. Although inquiry models exist for the study of teaching and teacher preparation, for the most part they are preliminary and tentative in nature.

    Recommendation. All inquiry models related to the study of teaching and teacher education should be identified, studied, and to the extent possible, verified and updated.

2. Research on effective schools, educational practices, and teaching offers findings that are promising, although some hold greater promise than others.

    Recommendation. All investigations related to effective schooling, educational practices, and teaching should be subjected to rigorous review by impartial observers to judge their reliability, validity, and generalizability. Further studies in these areas should be encouraged.

3. Some of the research findings on effective schooling, practices, and teaching square with what teachers do or say they believe; some do not.

    Recommendation. Special efforts must be made to encourage practitioners and policy makers to consider (with an open mind) promising practices that are not consistent with their beliefs and/or experiences.

4. Existing research has little to say about what constitutes effective teacher preparation. As far as could be determined, there are no studies that show definitive relationships between some form of professional preparation and effective classroom teaching. Thus teacher preparation programs, for the most part, are not empirically validated.

    Recommendation. Higher education institutions should validate their teacher preparation programs in rigorous ways related to the effectiveness of their graduates in the field.

5. Most research that informs teaching is fairly recent and appears in spurts, most likely reflecting political pressures for school improvement or perhaps because of the advent of new teaching methodologies and technology.

    Recommendation. Federal and state governments and foundations should make research that informs teaching and teacher preparation an ongoing priority.

6. In many cases, researchers seem unfamiliar with or choose not to mention related work conducted by others.

    Recommendation. A criterion for publication of research should be that the findings be discussed extensively in the light of related work of others. Further, primary investigators studying a certain variable should be identified and invited to contribute to a clearinghouse serving all related investigations. Each clearinghouse might serve as a repository of related research and would disseminate state-of-the-art papers, bibliographies, and other materials that would reinforce and extend related work in an organized, efficient manner.

7. There seem to be few investigators involved full time and over the long term in the subsets of research that inform teaching or teacher education. Rather, that research seems to be conducted by a cast of hundreds all playing bit parts.

   Recommendation. Faculty in doctoral-level and especially research center universities should be expected to declare an area of inquiry and to maintain it over an extended time. Whenever possible, they should guide their doctoral students in pursuing studies in their area of inquiry.

8. The research that informs teaching and teacher preparation varies greatly in quality and significance. There are many reasons for this, including the fact that some investigators are not well prepared to conduct studies.

   Recommendation. To ensure greater research competence, all candidates for the doctorate should attain a broad array of research competencies and should be mentored by faculty who themselves either conduct significant inquiry or teach research methodology.

These few observations and recommendations are made in the spirit of the purpose of this volume. Others in the research community might have other recommendations. But of one thing I am convinced: Teaching, schooling, and teacher preparation are vital human activities. As such, they call for the very best research effort.